8.07.2024

To Freddy, my
You are the mos
and fun person ₊ now.
Meeting you changed my life
in a positive way like I never
thought I would.
  With love, felicia ♡♡♡

Be yourself in your way

Strong, Bold, Inspired

Felicia Juliana Ursarescu

Copyright © 2024 Felicia Juliana Ursarescu
All rights reserved.
ISBN: 9798328511223

Independently published.

DEDICATION

This book is dedicated to my daughter, Iris Catalina.

Every moment spent with you is precious and fills me with happiness.

In you I have found absolute trust and unwavering support.

This book is proof of my gratitude to you.

I hope these pages are a tribute to our love and friendship.

In every word, you will find echoes of my affection and admiration for you.

With love and dedication, Mommy.

Contents

Introduction 6

How to get the most out of this book 9 6:24

Section: Me and Myself 11 11:06

Why Do I Feel Hungry Right Now? 12 11:12

What does my inner "garden" look like? 16 7:20:20

What new things am I discovering about myself? 19 26:07

If I were in your shoes... 23 34:03

Why am I feeling ashamed? 25 37:17

✓ Why on earth am I getting annoyed? 27 40:51

✱ How do I react to the unexpected? 29 44:28

When was the last time I truly listened to someone? 31 48:00 Interlocutor

What can I do to learn how to protect myself? 33 52:11

It's necessary... 35 55:34

How could I have been so foolish? 37 59:33

Do I believe I am God? 39 1:03:11

How do you communicate with your Vulnerable Inner Child? 41 1:06:58

If I don't see you, you don't exist! 43 1:10:55

What can you learn from this mistake? 45 1:14:48

What would I do if I had more time available? 47 1:11:32

Learn to master control! 49 1:22:25

How limited is your comfort zone? 51 1:26:01

○ What can I be thankful for today? 53 1:29:46

What makes you feel alive? 56 1:35:07

Did I celebrate myself? 58 1:38:52

How could I slow down a bit? 60 1:42:45

Make heaven out of what you have: your resources! 62 1:46:35

What makes me happy and fulfilled? 64 1:51:04 CAROLYN.

What is my body telling me? 66   1·54·56
What is my relationship with my energies? 68   1·58.35
The Free Inner Child 70   2.02·23
✷ If I had to tell a five-year-old, how would I say it? 72   2:06·01
What would I want to tell my teenage Self? 74   2:09·36
What do I want to change and why? 76   2:13·31
What can I do now to become the person I want to be? 78   2:17.27
Section: Me and Others 80   2:21.02
What do I see in the eyes of others? 81
✓ Envy, bitter fruit 83   2:25.30
The difference between a plain and a garden 85   2:28.39
With whom and what do I need to clarify? 87   2·32·21
The grass, the neighbour's goat, and the wife 89   2·36·02
With mask, without mask 91   2·39·39
My sacred space 93   2:43.16
Cast the first stone if you dare! 95   2:46.35
How can I make you understand that I love you? 97   2·49·26
Why do you ask yourself "why"? 99   2·52·47
When "no" actually means a resounding "YES" to the life we want 101   2·56·44
How well am I thriving in the garden I'm planted in? 103   3:00.53
✓ There will always be uncertainty and unpredictability. 105   3:04.29
Too much water can kill a flower. 107   3:07.58
Who am I when nobody is watching? 109   3·11.33
I dare to apologise 111   3·15·12
How do you receive compliments? 113   3·18·33
The legacy I leave behind. 115   3:21:53
In the end 117   3·25·39
Additional resources 119
About the author   3·29·46

Be yourself in your way

Introduction

> *" I've learned that you should live as if you were to die tomorrow. But also, you should learn as if you were to live forever."*
> *Maya Angelou*

Radiant soul,

I invite you on this journey towards the Self with an open heart, just as we gather, myself and the group I work with each month. In 'my tribe', we come together to share, learn, and grow, guided by collaboration and open-hearted listening, to learn the art of self-discovery and mindfulness - the art of living in the present, with all our awareness and attention.

The meetings and shared experiences have created a sense of belonging and communion that I wish to share with as many people as possible, hence the desire to write this book. It's a gift I want to offer you, whether you seek a moment of respite in the hustle and bustle of life or a way to reconnect with the small but essential things that bring joy and give meaning to life. Because we cannot belong to any tribe, we cannot feel the heart-to-heart connection unless we connect, accept, and know ourselves.

This book resembles a map to the hidden inner realms, indicating a path through the intricate layers of our psyche and our multifaceted relationships with others and, most importantly, with ourselves.

The journey to self-discovery is both challenging and beautiful. It is marked by revelations that unfold in moments of quiet introspection.

These pauses along the way are the ones in which we reconcile with the person we are and envision the person we aspire to be. This introspection is an inner dialogue, a sacred conversation with the Self, through which we lay the bricks of understanding and compassion that build the temple of our identity.

We cannot offer what we do not have.

I wrote this book for you who desire to take a moment for yourself, cultivate your attention, and truly listen to yourself. Within its pages, I will share the lessons I have learned so far and how you can practice mindfulness to bring more peace and balance into your life.

Together, we will explore how to better listen to our needs and take care of our souls when we are overwhelmed by stress and fatigue, whether in our daily work, in our relationships, or when we spend time alone, in the company of our thoughts.

I know that finding stability in this uncertain world can sometimes seem challenging. However, the journey back to yourself, to what you genuinely need, begins with small steps. And I am here to accompany you on this journey, step by step, with patience and understanding.

Setting aside moments for self-reflection is not just an act of self-care; it is a crucible for cultivating self-esteem. When we pause to reflect, we engage in love, recognising our worth and tending to our well-being. This commitment to self-awareness is the cornerstone of a healthy relationship with the Self, fostering an environment where trust can thrive, and self-esteem radiates.

Moreover, this "time for myself" is far from being selfish. Such moments of self-awareness allow us to return to the world more grounded and cantered. Self-knowledge profoundly transforms how we interact with others, enhancing our ability to understand and be understood. As we become more attuned to our inner world, our sensitivity to the world of others intensifies. We become channels of compassion, and our personal growth has a positive and lasting impact on our external relationships.

As we delve deeper into the journey within the pages of this book, we must consciously appreciate the awareness that by recognising and nurturing our value, we unintentionally transmit it to those around us. The journey of self-discovery opens our eyes to the kaleidoscope of human relationships. In these moments of self-reflection and through these pages of introspection, we permit ourselves to evolve - and in doing so, we invite the world to evolve alongside us.

May this book be for you a true friend, a companion who whispers gently to you what the next step is to live consciously and be present in every moment. Together, let us discover the joy of returning to ourselves, "home," whenever necessary.

With warmth and openness, I thank you for joining me in this journey of discovery and mindfulness. Let our adventure towards heart and presence begin.

May my thoughts of peace and harmony find you, wherever you may be,

Felicia - Rivadu

How to get the most out of this book

Firstly, let's see if this book is right for you. Can it help you on your journey towards self-discovery? Can it be useful for your inner peace and harmony with yourself and others?

Mark the questions you answer with a yes:

- ○ I feel that I am more easily overwhelmed by emotions or feel them more intensely than others.
- ○ Sometimes, I have impulsive reactions that harm myself or others.
- ○ I struggle with motivating myself to complete what I start.
- ○ My relationships have a lot of conflicts or ups and downs.
- ○ I feel like I'm living life on autopilot.
- ○ I often feel overwhelmed by what is happening in my life.
- ○ Sometimes, even the most minor things can change my mood or ruin my day.

If you answered "yes" to more than three statements, I believe this book can be helpful to you. When you're on a journey by car, it's crucial to have a map to figure out where you are and how to get to where you want to go best. Consider this introduction a map for your journey alongside me!

I wrote this book in the form of bibliotherapy, a type of structured self-help book in psychology designed to help those struggling with mental health difficulties to "self-treat" without seeking a therapist.

The book consists of 49 chapters. At the end of each chapter are "homework assignments" to practice a new skill. I recommend reading each chapter (including the exercises) in a single session whenever possible, as some exercises include more detailed descriptions. Additionally, some exercises are much easier to understand after practising them.

Some exercises may take only a minute, while others take more than 15 minutes. I encourage you to keep a dedicated journal to reflect more deeply on your experiences and what you learn.

The order of the chapters is intentional. Each new insight builds on the others and overlaps with them, so this book is meant to be read and used in the presented order.

For your personal growth journey, I urge you to prioritise self-care and self-reflection. This book is a tool to guide you, but it's up to you to take the steps. Read the entire book and do each exercise - you'll never know what's useful until you try, sometimes even more than once.

Second, schedule dedicated time for this book if you can. It will help you prioritise your work with yourself if you plan your reading and homework each week.

Third, it is crucial to think about ways to support and reward yourself. Recognise and address your emotional and physical needs. You could create a mantra for when things get tough, share what you discover about yourself with a friend, or schedule self-care activities to reward yourself after completing your homework.

What should you do after finishing this book?

You can read the entire book again! You'll gain a different level of understanding about yourself and discover new aspects. Additionally, I've included suggestions at the end of the book for further self-exploration: books, podcasts, websites, and other resources.

In conclusion, I'd like you to start this journey with self-compassion. Remember, everyone does the best they can. Often, when people struggle to change a behaviour, they blame themselves. "I'm not doing enough" is a statement I often hear from the people I work with. But it's not an excellent way to get to know and befriend parts of ourselves. Be kind, be friendly, and be gentle with yourself. With this attitude, let's begin the journey!

Section: Me and Myself

Why Do I Feel Hungry Right Now?

> " *You can't stop the waves, but you can learn to surf on them.*"
> *Jon Kabat-Zinn, Emeritus Professor of Medicine and creator of the Mindfulness-Based Stress Reduction program*

In a world where speed and efficiency are often the most coveted values, we find ourselves prisoners of our own frantic pace of life. We become hamsters on a wheel that isn't even ours.

We rush from one responsibility to another, cramming our schedules with tasks and activities without assessing what is truly important to us. This way of life can leave us exhausted, without realising what we genuinely miss or what we could do to improve the quality of our lives. In this continuous tumult, we often lose contact with our needs and desires, forgetting to listen to our body and soul.

The question „Why do I feel 'hungry' right now?" isn't just metaphorical.

It indicates the need to reevaluate our priorities and focus on what truly matters. Being constantly busy, we often ignore the signals of our body that are asking for a break, forget to eat on time or to hydrate properly, take a breath of fresh air, or give ourselves a moment of relaxation, creativity, or "dolce far niente" as the Italians say. These are the last things on our crowded "to-do" list. And being the last, we never get around to doing them.

In addition to physical needs, we ignore the emotional signals of our need for connection with others. A hug from a loved one, a quiet moment spent with a friend, or a sincere conversation offering clarity and emotional support are often sacrificed on the altar of „productivity" and „efficiency" because we have learned to suppress our emotional needs. Emotional needs are incompatible with the „efficiency" that we demand.

The initial step is to recognise and name our needs to regain balance and improve our quality of life. This means giving ourselves time to converse with ourselves, listen to our body and heart, and identify what is missing and what could make us feel better. 'Naming our needs' refers to identifying and acknowledging our physical, emotional, and psychological needs, a crucial step in self-awareness and self-care.

By naming our needs, we become more aware of them and take the first step towards meeting them. For example, if we realise that we are hungry for a break, it might be time to rearrange our day to include moments of relaxation. If we feel the need for food even when our stomach is full, or if we feel the need for alcohol, cigarettes, or other recreational drugs (including social media), it is a signal that we need to reflect more deeply on our unmet emotional needs. These could include the need for connection, relaxation, or emotional support. The need for a hug may indicate a lack of connection and affection, requiring a conscious effort to spend more quality time with loved ones.

By listening to and naming our needs, we improve our well-being and equip ourselves with the means to build a more balanced and fulfilling life.

Ultimately, it's not just about surviving the whirlwind of hectic life but about genuinely learning to live, appreciating every moment, and responding carefully to what our body and soul ask of us. In a broader sense, naming our needs is an act of courage and authenticity, as we acknowledge that we are vulnerable human beings with real needs that deserve attention and care.

Practising this simple yet profound gesture helps us establish healthy boundaries, allowing us to say „no" when it's too much and „yes" to things that bring us joy and health. For instance, a boundary of not working on weekends can help us prioritise rest and leisure, leading to a better work-life balance and improved well-being. It also helps us develop compassion for ourselves and others, becoming more understanding and patient with our own and others' imperfections.

Naming our needs is the first step toward a more conscious and fulfilling life. It's an invitation to slow down, to turn our gaze inward, and to give ourselves what we truly need.

When we succeed, we improve the quality of our lives and become a positive example for those around us, showing that living in harmony with ourselves and the world is possible.

I invite you to reflect: Why do I feel "hungry" right now?

Do we need a break, food, coffee, a hug, or clarifications? Beginning to name our needs is the first step to fulfilling them.

If you haven't practised mindfulness before and you're someone who's learned to be „on the fast track", start with 5 minutes. Even 1 minute is fine.

After you read the exercise, set the book aside and do it. Don't move on to the next chapter unless you've done this simple exercise at least once. There's no rush; you don't have to get anywhere, and you can resist the curiosity to find out what's on the next page!

The exercise is simple, but the more you practice it, the more you develop the ability to listen to yourself and connect with your needs.

Sit in a comfortable position. It doesn't matter if you're in the lotus or another trendy position. What's important is that you feel as comfortable as possible. Close your eyes and focus on yourself. What do you think this „self" means? You can start by focusing on the body. Feel it. Feel if it expresses any pain, discomfort, or a message. Maybe there's a part of the body twitching or moving. Do you think it's random? Talk to that part. Listen to it. Ask it what it's doing here, what it wants from you. Then, stay silent, without judging, without labelling, without expectations. And accept the answer in whatever form it may come: an image, a thought, a memory, a long-forgotten desire.

Then, go further. Focus on that point you consider the centre of your being.

Whatever this point may be. Ask yourself: *"Where is the centre of my being?"* And wait patiently. You will indeed receive the answer, but sometimes it may surprise you. Some people feel that the centre of their being is in their hearts, others in their stomachs. And that's okay. It can be. But perhaps, in one of your explorations, you may receive a different answer. For example, maybe at this moment, the centre of your being is in the little toe of your left foot. It may surprise you, and you may instinctively reject such a message. Accept it. And stay tuned. *What else does it have to tell you? What does it want now? What are the unheard needs? What are the unexpressed desires?* Listen. Ask: *"Why do I feel hungry now?"* Listen. Then, ask yourself again. And listen, listen... You will receive the answers. You need to be patient without expectations.

And you finish this conscious self-exploration and feel that the process is complete (not when you lose patience because you feel the uncontrollable need to check your phone), open your eyes and jot down in your journal, without judgment, the answer, or answers. And think about how you could satisfy this hunger. The more you practice this exercise, the more exciting answers you will receive.

Aren't you curious?

Be yourself in your way, Strong, Bold, Inspired

What does my inner "garden" look like?

"Within every soul lies an inner garden, which must be tended with one's own hands."

Marcus Tullius Cicerone

In a world marked by the pursuit of success and the constant pressure of time, our tendency is always to look ahead and plan the next step, often ignoring the signals we receive from within. We are taught to evaluate and judge rather than to feel and listen. It seems so simple and obvious to know what we feel, yet, unfortunately, this essential skill of self-observation is often neglected or underestimated.

We may have reached a point where we have completely lost the habit of asking ourselves, „*How do I feel?*"—not because we don't care, but because the pace of life prevents us from stopping our endless race. We might even be trapped in the belief that our emotions are unimportant or that reflecting on them is a luxury we cannot afford.

However, stopping for a few seconds right now to take a „snapshot" of your inner „garden" is not just an act of courage but also one of profound self-care. In guided meditations, whether in individual sessions or group sessions, I use this metaphor of the „inner garden". The concept is not new; Cicero used it more than 2000 years ago. The „inner garden" concept is a profound metaphor for our inner life—our emotions, thoughts, and spirit. Just as a real garden requires care, attention, and constant work to bloom and bear fruit, so too does our inner garden need time, dedication, and consideration to thrive. This concept evokes the idea that we are responsible for our emotional and psychological well-being, and how we manage our inner life can significantly influence the quality of our life experiences.

When you stop to observe inwardly, to observe your "inner garden", what do you find there? Perhaps, for a moment, you feel like you are on the verge of discovering an unknown territory. Maybe right from the start, you feel bursts of joy manifesting as relief, serenity, or even a quiet excitement for something that is about to happen or something you have accomplished.

You might also encounter less comfortable feelings such as anger or frustration in the same inner landscape. These may arise in response to unresolved situations, interpersonal conflicts, or external pressures. Acknowledging their presence can already be a first step in managing these emotions.

Sadness can also appear in the inner garden. It might be a vague, undefined sadness, or it might be related to a specific event. Accepting that it also has a place within us without rushing to dismiss or judge it is important.

Pause now and contemplate this range of emotions as a complex and colourful landscape. Consider how each feeling influences you, your decisions, and your interactions with others. By better understanding your emotions and how they affect you, you may discover new ways of responding to situations.

Exploring your inner garden, you begin to know yourself better. This self-awareness is not just about accepting the wide range of emotions you can experience but also about equipping yourself with the ability to navigate through and with them. By learning to recognise and name what you feel, you can start responding more consciously and deliberately, rather than reacting impulsively or suppressing emotions.

Regularly pausing to reflect on your inner state can become a valuable part of your self-care routine. It may start with a few seconds or minutes each day, but the beneficial effects will accumulate over time, leading to greater harmony between mind, body, and emotions. This conscious effort of self-exploration improves your well-being and can enrich your relationships with others, allowing you to show up in the world with a stronger foundation of understanding and compassion, both for yourself and others.

Ultimately, every step taken in listening to our inner state is a step toward a more conscious and fulfilling life. It's a journey that begins by acknowledging that every emotion, no matter how small or large, plays a role in shaping our human experience.

I invite you to reflect:

It seems obvious to KNOW what we feel, but often, we don't even take five minutes a day to listen. Maybe we've lost the habit of asking ourselves, and maybe we don't even know. It doesn't matter. Stop now for a few seconds to explore your inner garden: What do you notice it to be?

Joy? Anger? Perhaps sadness? Or something else?

Breathe. Observe. Breathe. Observe. Breathe. Observe. See. Acknowledge.

Be yourself in your way, Strong, Bold, Inspired

What new things am I discovering about myself?

" There is no awareness without pain."
Carl Gustav Jung

When we experience an unpleasant or difficult experience, our initial reaction is often to seek an escape route. We are programmed to avoid discomfort and pain, whether physical, emotional, or mental suffering. When we feel guilty about past events, we tend to get lost in reproaches and regrets without constructively valuing these moments. This approach, though perfectly understandable from a human standpoint, often deprives us of the opportunity to grow and find meaning in the difficulties encountered.

Learning and personal development are possible only when we accept and confront these experiences rather than avoid or be overwhelmed by them. Even the most painful moments bring valuable lessons that can help us evolve as individuals. Actively questioning "What can I learn from this experience?" represents an essential first step in recovery and understanding.

Reflecting on this question can reveal the perspective and resilience needed to navigate difficulties. It may uncover, for example, unknown capacities for adaptability and inner strength, or it can help us make choices and change behaviours. In every mistake or failure, there lies an opportunity to learn something valuable about us, our relationships with others, and the surrounding world.

Furthermore, approaching difficult experiences with an attitude of curiosity and openness, we begin to cultivate compassion towards ourselves. We learn to treat ourselves with the same gentleness and understanding that we would offer to a dear friend in a similar situation. This self-compassion process helps us overcome guilt and self-criticism, providing us with the space needed for healing and growth.

Moreover, by exploring and embracing the lessons learned from difficult experiences, we better prepare ourselves for future challenges. Responding to life situations with greater emotional maturity and improved coping skills becomes easier. Therefore, the question "What can I learn from this experience?" becomes a tool for managing difficult moments and a catalyst for personal development and long-term wisdom.

By reminding ourselves to ask what we can learn from each experience, we open the path to a more conscious and fulfilling life, where every moment, whether pleasant or challenging, is valued as an opportunity for growth. This process of questioning and answering empowers us to live with deeper meaning, cultivate resilience, and build a more positive and compassionate relationship with ourselves. Ultimately, the ability to extract lessons from every situation we encounter is not just about survival but about "flourishing and yielding results" in the most authentic and fulfilling ways possible, consistent with who we are at our core.

I invite you to reflect:

When we go through an unpleasant or difficult experience, we often wish to do everything to escape from it. Or we continue to struggle with guilt for something that didn't go well in the past. But by doing so, we don't help ourselves at all. Something about ourselves always needs to be retrieved or understood from our experiences. Useful questions to ask yourself in such situations are:

- ✓ What can I learn from this experience?
- ✓ What new skills help me discover?
- ✓ What new things do I discover about myself through this experience?

If you're currently going through a challenging experience in your life, take a moment of silence and reflect on the situation. If you're not experiencing a difficult situation, recall the last one you went through. Your initial reaction might be to flee from that pain. This "flight" can manifest in different ways: your mind wanders off, you suddenly remember an urgent task, you feel hungry or thirsty out of nowhere, you crave something sweet, or you want a cigarette. You check who has posted what on social media, etc. Make a conscious effort to stay with yourself and the discomfort. Practice "letting go" and then reflect on the above questions.

"Letting go" is gently releasing what no longer serves us. It invites us to merge with the present moment, relaxing our body and calming our mind. There are many ways to explore this notion of release. The following practice is an essential body scan that incorporates our intention to relinquish what no longer serves us. Explore it with curiosity, openness, patience, and compassion.

Here is my suggestion:

1. Lie down in a comfortable reclining position, supported on your back, with your spine straight. Your arms and legs can comfortably rest on the supporting surface. Take five to ten grounding breaths, and then direct your attention to the crown of your head.

2. As you slowly scan your body from head to toe, notice any areas of tension you encounter (including thoughts). Whenever you experience a particular type of tension, take a few deep breaths in that area (or in that thought). As you inhale, whisper silently to yourself: "I see you. " As you exhale, whisper silently to yourself: "I surrender".

3. Continue to be a witness and breathe attentively while whispering:

I see you... I surrender.

I see you... I surrender.

4. After scanning your entire body, keep your entire being in awareness as you ground yourself through breathing for a few more minutes. Repeat the same affirmations with each breath if other thoughts or feelings arise that are eager to be let go.

5. Return to the present moment When you feel the practice is complete. When you feel ready to do so, open your eyes.

Now, reflect on the three questions and jot down your answers in your journal.

Important: "Letting go" isn't a practice we undertake just because we've told ourselves we want to release something. It's a process that takes varying amounts of time, depending on what we're letting go of and many other factors.

In cases of trauma, it's recommended to collaborate with a mental health professional. Additionally, this isn't a practice meant to replace medication for serious health issues.

Additional practices facilitating the letting go process include progressive muscle relaxation (body scan), mindful journaling, diaphragmatic breathing, and visualisation.

Be yourself in your way, Strong, Bold, Inspired

If I were in your shoes...

> *" It seems easier to give good advice than to follow it."*
> Lucius Annaeus Seneca

When faced with difficult situations, getting lost in the maze of our thoughts, emotions, and experiences is easy. We often feel overwhelmed, powerless, or confused and turn against ourselves, criticising how we handle the situation. This habit of being too immersed in our experience can make finding solutions or a way out of the problem harder. We're so caught up in our own „painting" that we no longer see the whole „puzzle, " the big picture.

In contrast, when we look at the lives or situations of others, we have the advantage of distance. This external perspective allows us to observe details that the person might not see and to offer objective advice or encouragement based on a broader understanding of the context.

This dynamic reveals a proper lesson about human nature and how we process experiences. Despite the difficulty of „stepping out of our own story, "viewing our problems from someone else's perspective can be extraordinarily liberating and therapeutic. By attempting to visualise our problems as if they belonged to a close friend, we could see solutions we hadn't considered before and treat ourselves with more compassion and understanding.

Reflecting on the stories of others also teaches us about human resilience and adaptability. Observing how others have navigated their tribulations can inspire us and give us the strength to face our difficulties. Additionally, it reminds us that we are not alone in our struggles, which can provide us with an added sense of comfort and hope.

We can practice mindfulness and self-reflection to cultivate this ability to distance ourselves from our own experiences and analyse them from a more objective perspective. Additionally, it is helpful to openly discuss our issues with others because, through sharing experiences, we help each other discover solutions that we may not individually notice.

So, the ability to reflect on the experiences of others and apply this perspective to our situations can be a valuable tool for navigating life's complexities. It can help us better understand ourselves and find effective solutions to our problems.

I invite you to reflect: Often, we're so involved and immersed in our own experience that we lose the bigger picture. Instead, it's easier to reflect on others and their stories.

Now, for a moment, healthily distance yourself from your own experience: What would you recommend if you were looking at yourself through the eyes of someone who loves you?

Be yourself in your way, Strong, Bold, Inspired

Why am I feeling ashamed?

> " *Shame is a profound soul feeling, deeper than any other sentiment. Through shame, the infinite is reflected in the finite.*"
> Søren Kierkegaard

Although often perceived as a profoundly negative and challenging emotion, shame can be a valuable introspective tool. This sharp and undoubtedly unpleasant sensation can signal and behaviours or actions may not fully align with the values or standards we hold dear. In this sense, shame can function as an internal moral compass, prompting us to reassess and adjust how we present ourselves and interact in the world.

When experiencing shame, it's usually a sign that we've done something that inherently feels like it undermines our image or identity in the eyes of others and, most importantly, in our own eyes. Many situations can trigger this feeling, from minor mistakes to severe moral transgressions. The paradoxical and profoundly human aspect of shame reflects our intense desire to belong, be accepted, and be appreciated by our community and society.

Therefore, shame invites us to turn inward and identify the personal aspects that have led us to experience this emotion. It stimulates us to ask relevant questions about the reasons why specific actions or behaviours make us feel this way, as well as about our values or expectations that we feel we've violated. This process of self-exploration can reveal discrepancies between how we perceive ourselves and how we want to be perceived, paving the way for authentic and meaningful personal development.

The emphasis here is on transforming shame from a paralysing force into a mobilising one. Instead of allowing this emotion to sink us into a spiral of self-judgment and self-doubt, we can choose to see it as a catalyst for change and personal growth. By learning from moments of shame and approaching them with an open mind and a willingness to improve, we can use these experiences as pivot points to become better versions of ourselves, more aligned with our core values.

Thus, despite the discomfort it entails, shame holds a valuable core of truth and opportunity. When approached with compassion and a genuine desire to learn from it, shame can become a passage to self-awareness and personal transformation, allowing us to align with who we truly want to be.

I invite you to reflect: Shame is a sharp and unpleasant emotion, yet highly useful: it helps us discover those aspects of ourselves that we feel are met with disapproval or judgment, especially from ourselves. Pay attention to what you're ashamed of, and then ask yourself:

- ✓ Why/Who am I ashamed of?
- ✓ What can I do to soothe my inner judge?

Be yourself in your way, Strong, Bold, Inspired

Why on earth am I getting annoyed?

"Anger, if not controlled, often harms us more than the injury that caused it."

Lucius Annaeus Seneca

Anger is often negatively labelled and seen as an emotion to avoid or repress. However, like any other emotion, anger has a vital purpose and can be surprisingly useful if understood and appropriately managed. It serves as an alarm signal indicating that something is wrong, that we feel wronged, or that our needs and rights are not adequately respected. It is one of the most common emotions encountered by the people I work with, which is no coincidence.

Anger manifests in different ways, from mild irritation to intense rage, and the emotional response can vary depending on the person and the context. Regardless of how it appears, this emotion is crucial in alerting us to situations where our boundaries are being violated or our core values are being challenged. It acts as a self-defence mechanism, prompting us to recognise and address the issues affecting our well-being.

Moreover, anger allows us to focus on personal aspects or needs that haven't been adequately protected or appreciated by others. It signals that we need to pay more attention to our integrity and learn to assert what is important to us constructively. In this sense, anger can guide us to set clearer boundaries and communicate more effectively with those around us, healthily expressing our needs and expectations.

Instead of seeing anger as an emotion to avoid or repress, it is helpful to recognise it as a valuable indicator that helps us identify the problems we face. By understanding the source of our anger and learning to express it balanced, we can use this emotion to catalyse personal growth and improve our relationships with others.

Effective anger management involves developing emotional regulation and conflict resolution skills, allowing us to address problems proactively and turn potential tensions into opportunities for dialogue and mutual understanding. Thus, when correctly managed, anger reveals its true potential: to be a powerful tool for self-awareness, self-assertion, and personal transformation.

I invite you to reflect: Anger, like all emotions, is very useful, but it has a very bad reputation. Its role is to alert us to experiences we perceive as unjust, those in which our needs and rights have not been recognised by others. It allows us to highlight aspects of ourselves that have not been seen and respected (by others) and demands that we learn to do this for ourselves.

- ✓ When you encounter this emotion, ask yourself:
- ✓ Why am I getting angry?
- ✓ How can I use my anger?
- ✓ What can I do to make others respect my boundaries?
- ✓ What can I do to be seen and heard?

Be yourself in your way, Strong, Bold, Inspired

How do I react to the unexpected?

> *" It's not what happens to you that matters, but how you choose to react to what happens to you."*
>
> *Lucius Annaeus Seneca*

In life's vast and complex journey, we often encounter situations imposed upon us, either by circumstances or the dynamics of relationships with others. Some of these experiences can be challenging, painful, or even disappointing. They can take various forms—from losing a loved one to unexpected changes in career or health issues. In such moments, we are reminded of a fundamental reality: we do not always have control over what happens to us.

However, amidst unpredictability and often chaos, one element remains within our control: our attitude towards what we experience. This is perhaps one of the most powerful choices at our disposal and, simultaneously, one of the most challenging. Our attitude shapes our perception of life's experiences, influences how we respond to them, and ultimately, can determine the trajectory of recovery or personal growth.

To choose to face difficulties with resilience and optimism does not mean denying reality or the difficulty of the situation, but rather acknowledging that, despite the trials, there is a strength within you capable of enduring, adapting, and seeking solutions or positive aspects even where it seems only darkness. This attitude involves viewing each challenge as an opportunity for growth, learning, and personal development.

Additionally, approaching challenging situations with compassion and understanding towards yourself and those involved can ease your emotional burden. Practising empathy and tolerance can help you navigate through tense situations, maintain your inner balance, and strengthen your relationships with those around you.

The attitude of gratitude in the face of adversity is another transformative choice. Even in the darkest moments, attempting to identify elements, no matter how small, for which you can be grateful can change the emotional dynamics of the experience and help you maintain a balanced perspective in the face of difficulties.

Essentially, the attitude we choose in the face of life's unforeseen experiences defines our character and determines the quality of our lives. By cultivating an attitude based on resilience, compassion, gratitude, and optimism, we can enrich our existence even in the face of unknown and inevitable challenges. Thus, even though we may not always choose life's circumstances, we can always choose how to face them.

I invite you to reflect: There are life experiences that we cannot choose and that are beyond our control. However, there is always something we can still choose to experience.

- ✓ What attitude do I choose to approach them with?
- ✓ What can I do to live with them in a way that is sustainable for me?

Be yourself in your way, Strong, Bold, Inspired

When was the last time I truly listened to someone?

*"Listen with the intention to understand,
not with the intention to respond."*
Stephen R. Covey

In the frenetic pace of contemporary life, where days seem to pass by too quickly, and everyone's agenda is overloaded with tasks and responsibilities, the art of authentic listening becomes increasingly rare. We are often too preoccupied with our thoughts, plans, and concerns, so deep and sincere communication moments seem a rarity. The need to be truly listened to by others, if neglected (intentionally or unintentionally), significantly impacts the quality of our relationships.

When we practice active listening, we not only hear the words being spoken but, in a much broader sense, consider the speaker's feelings, experiences, and perspectives. This form of listening involves letting go of our own biases, being open to what is being communicated, and being authentically present in the conversation. It is a gesture of deep consideration and respect that confirms the value of our interlocutor.

The impact of authentic listening on relational dynamics is significant. Truly listening creates a space of safety for openness and vulnerability, allowing those involved to express themselves without fear of judgment. This level of communicative intimacy can lead to a better understanding of the other person and a better self-awareness.

Within these exchanges, we not only encounter the stories and experiences of others, but also our values, thoughts, and emotions are reflected. In this way, listening becomes a tool for personal enrichment and an opportunity to honour our conversation partner.

Furthermore, this openness fostered by authentic listening facilitates empathy and compassion. By being receptive to others' experiences, we can see the world from their perspective, understand the depth of their emotions, and appreciate the context in which they act. This form of human connection is essential for building a more understanding and united society.

The practice of authentic listening demands that we slow down, set aside our thoughts and concerns, and offer our full attention to the speaker. It is undoubtedly a challenge in a world that values speed and efficiency, but its benefits for the quality of relationships and personal fulfilment are immeasurable. By reclaiming the art of listening, we rediscover not only our ability to connect with others in meaningful ways but also ourselves and the vastness of our inner selves.

I invite you to reflect. Often, we rush too quickly without truly listening to those around us. When we genuinely listen, we feel the difference: a closeness so profound that we learn more about the other person's story and ourselves.

- ✓ I ask you to observe yourself while interacting with someone, whether it's the cashier at the supermarket, your child, or your boss. Be present with your thoughts and your way of listening actively or passively.

- ✓ Do you wish for them to finish quickly so you can share your opinion? Are you patient enough to listen until the end, or do you quickly jump to conclusions and personal opinions?

- ✓ Besides the conversation topic, what else can you learn by listening to that person?

Be yourself in your way, Strong, Bold, Inspired

What can I do to learn how to protect myself?

> *"It's not that I'm not afraid. But I've trained myself to confront my fear."*
> Nelson Mandela

Discovering what we fear is a crucial step in exploring the depths of ourselves. Although fear is often seen as an enemy or obstacle, it is an important signal that our body and mind send us. This signal informs us that we are facing something perceived as potentially dangerous or harmful. When we become aware of what triggers our fear, we allow ourselves to connect with the most vulnerable part of our being.

This vulnerability should not be seen as a weakness but rather, just like the emotions explored so far, as an opportunity to grow and learn. Protecting this vulnerable part essentially means developing adaptation mechanisms to circumstances that allow us to cope with difficult situations in healthy and constructive ways rather than through avoidance or denial.

Our instinctive reactions to fear—flight, fight, or freeze—are primitive survival mechanisms that served our ancestors in environments full of various dangers. However, in the modern context, these responses are often inappropriate and can amplify fear instead of resolving it. For example, constantly avoiding what we fear can limit our experiences and hinder personal growth. The "fight" attitude can generate conflicts and damage relationships, while "freezing" can lead to missing out on significant opportunities.

Understanding and accepting fear as part of the human experience is vital. By investigating the source of our fears, we can learn specific strategies to manage them. This process requires time, patience, and often, the courage to confront aspects of life that cause us discomfort. Therapy, self-reflection journals, mindfulness techniques, and meditation are just a few tools that can assist in this journey.

As we learn to protect and care for our vulnerable parts, we may discover an unexpected source of inner strength. This is, after all, the paradox of fear: by facing it, we give ourselves an opportunity for growth and evolution that we might otherwise have missed. Thus, ultimately, discovering and protecting our vulnerability transforms fear from an obstacle into a valuable ally in the personal development journey.

I invite you to reflect. Discovering what we fear helps us connect with our most vulnerable part and invites us to learn how to protect it. When we're afraid, we react by fleeing, fighting, or freezing, amplifying fear.

- ✓ Why am I afraid? What can I do to learn how to protect myself?

- ✓ What if, when you're afraid, you stop to listen to yourself? To listen to fear instead of running from it.

Be yourself in your way, Strong, Bold, Inspired

It's necessary...

> *" In 20 years from now, you will be more disappointed by the things you didn't do than by the ones you did. So, unfurl the sails. Sail away from the safe harbour. Catch the strong winds. Explore. Dream. Discover."*
>
> *Mark Twain*

The inner dialogue we maintain with ourselves is essential in perceiving ourselves and the reality around us. These inner conversations can be harsh and even malicious, reflecting standards we impose on ourselves or believe society expects us to adhere to. Phrases like „I must rely only on my strength," „I must be strong and grit my teeth, " or „I must not be afraid" are expectations that can exert enormous pressure on us.

This constant predisposition towards a "tough guy" attitude and the demeanour of always being on guard, strong, and unyielding may conceal a deep fear of vulnerability. Showing oneself as solid and unshakable may seem like a good shield against external or even our judgment. However, this attitude can become suffocating and, ironically, can amplify feelings of loneliness and isolation because it distances us from our true humanity, including vulnerability, fluctuating emotions, and the need for support.

But what happens if we can't constantly maintain this facade of power and control? What if we can't "grit our teeth" anymore?

Accepting that we are not always strong, that sometimes we are afraid, and that we cannot always predict or control everything can be a first step towards greater self-compassion. Recognising our vulnerability is not a sign of weakness but an indication of the courage to be authentic and human. Instead of forcing ourselves to meet these high and often unrealistic standards, we can try to treat ourselves with more kindness and permit ourselves not to be perfect.

Being kinder to ourselves also means learning to manage failures and frustrations with a constructive attitude rather than harsh self-criticism. Instead of suppressing or denying fears and negative emotions, we can explore and understand them, allowing us to develop healthier coping strategies and improve our relationship with ourselves and others.

Being open to our vulnerability also means being open to deep and meaningful human connections because authenticity attracts authenticity. Therefore, admitting that sometimes we are not as strong and that we need support not only helps us feel less alone but also allows us to build relationships based on honesty and trust. Letting go of the need to be strong and unyielding can open the path to a more fulfilling and balanced life.

I invite you to reflect: In today's world, we have our way of talking to ourselves; sometimes it's a harsh conversation: „I must rely solely on my strength", „I must be strong and grit my teeth", „I must give my all and strive", „I must not be afraid", „I must understand and be able to predict/control everything", etc.

Each of us has our methods of pushing ourselves and coping. Often, these become defence mechanisms to not listen to anything else: what happens if... you're not strong and don't grit your teeth?

What is the most recurring "obligation" I struggle with?

Be yourself in your way, Strong, Bold, Inspired

How could I have been so foolish?

> *"Critique yourself, but never discourage yourself."*
> Ralph Waldo Emerson

Our inner dialogue in moments of failure or mistake is an open window to our relationship with ourselves and to our perception of ourselves. The way we address ourselves in such moments can provide revealing clues about our relationship with ourselves, about how much self-respect we possess, and, in a broader sense, about how we have been shaped by early experiences and relationships in our lives.

When we make mistakes, we are often tempted to harshly self-criticize. Phrases like "How could I be so stupid? " or "I'm a failure" are signs of a tense and critical inner relationship. This severe self-condemnation only undermines self-esteem and fuels a vicious cycle of negativity, which may have roots in how we were criticised or punished in the past for our mistakes, especially in childhood.

Children treated harshly or frequently blamed tend to develop an equally harsh and limiting inner dialogue. In recent years, I have dedicated myself to working with the Inner Child Wound, and what is striking is that everyone who has been treated harshly and criticised in childhood has developed a fierce Inner Critic and Judge.

On the other hand, treating ourselves with compassion and understanding in the face of mistakes, adopting an attitude like "It's okay to make mistakes; we all make them. What's important is to learn from them," reflects a healthy and constructive inner relationship. This approach stems from an upbringing and early relationships marked by acceptance, understanding, and support, which have fostered an internal sense of security and self-acceptance.

Self-compassion and self-listening are indicators of a quality relationship with us. They are ways in which we recover after a mistake, no matter how "big" it may be, and evolve, largely defining the quality of the emotional life we experience.

The importance of these moments cannot be underestimated, as they have the power to shape our relationships with ourselves and influence our interactions with others. How we treat ourselves in moments of vulnerability also projects how we will respond to the weaknesses and mistakes of others, whether they be partners, friends, or colleagues.

Essentially, what we tell ourselves when we make mistakes is a barometer of self-understanding and self-compassion. This internal dialogue is also a starting point for self-awareness and personal growth, a signal of the work we can do to heal and improve our relationships with ourselves and, implicitly, with the world around us.

I invite you to reflect:

What we tell ourselves when we make mistakes says a lot about how we know to treat ourselves, the quality of our relationship with ourselves, and our history of how we have been treated.

- ✓ Bring your attention to what you tell yourself when you make mistakes.

- ✓ Is there something different you would like to tell yourself?

- ✓ How would you like to support yourself? How could you support yourself?

Be yourself in your way, Strong, Bold, Inspired

Do I believe I am God?

> *"The person who tries to carry too many heavy burdens may end up losing them all."* - Esopus

The tendency to take on a disproportionate amount of responsibility that is not realistic or healthy is a common trait among many individuals, especially those who identify with the role of "saviour" in their personal or professional lives. On the one hand, this can be a quality that demonstrates commitment and a desire to provide support. Still, on the other hand, it can contribute to exhaustion, stress, and disillusionment when they encounter the harsh reality that some situations are beyond their control.

Believing that every situation depends solely on our ability to control, solve, or prevent problems can be a psychological trap. This mindset leaves us imprisoned in a world where pressure and disappointment become frequent experiences, especially in the face of circumstances that are inherently unpredictable or dependent on the actions and choices of others.

Many aspects of life are simply beyond our control. Whether it's the behaviour of other people, unforeseen events, or the complex dynamics of certain situations, there are natural and healthy limits to what we can influence. Recognizing and accepting this truth doesn't mean giving up on our responsibility or commitment but rather embracing a more balanced and realistic approach to life.

By learning to distinguish between what we can control and what we cannot, we can adopt a healthier attitude towards responsibility. This often involves setting healthy boundaries, practising delegation, and accepting perfection as an intangible ideal.

It's also important to trust those around us, acknowledging that they, too, can contribute valuable input to resolving a situation. Embracing uncertainty and cultivating resilience can help us navigate life's complexities with greater inner peace. Instead of overly focusing on aspects we cannot control, we can choose to emphasize how we respond and adapt to what life brings us.

In conclusion, while the desire to take control and resolve situations may be deeply rooted in good intentions, it's essential to recognise our limitations. This not only protects us from overwhelm and disappointment but also provides an opportunity to build healthier relationships, based on trust, honesty, and acceptance, both with ourselves and with others.

I invite you to reflect: We often tend to overload ourselves with responsibility, thinking that a certain situation depends solely on us. Perhaps we want to control it, solve it, or prevent problems. But often, this doesn't work because there are things that don't depend on us!

- ✓ Stop for a moment and try to distinguish what depends on you and what you can do from what doesn't depend on you and, therefore, what you can't do. Honestly, answer:
- ✓ What depends on me in this experience?
- ✓ What doesn't depend on me?

Be yourself in your way, Strong, Bold, Inspired

How do you communicate with your Vulnerable Inner Child?

> " *In every adult, there is a child, and deep within every child, there is an adult.*" - Richard Rohr

Being harsh on ourselves in times of difficulty is a behaviour many of us develop as an innate response to failure or challenge. This harsh self-criticism can stem from internal beliefs, expectations, and external influences such as parental upbringing, societal pressures, or professional standards. We treat ourselves with severity based on the idea that perfectionism and constant self-monitoring will push us to grow. However, this often hinders our growth and brings us into a cycle of negativity.

This tendency to be harsh on ourselves often has its roots in the messages we receive in childhood. If parents or caregivers use harsh criticism as a form of motivation, we may internalize this critical voice as our own way of self-guidance. This mental model is based on the belief that only through constant self-monitoring and harsh criticism can we achieve desired accomplishments.

Unfortunately, our internal critical behaviour can affect our self-esteem, induce anxiety, and make us never feel good enough, no matter how hard we try. Instead of motivating us, this harshness can paralyze us, leading us to avoid challenges to avoid failure, criticism, and self-criticism that may follow. Thus, opportunities for learning and growth are lost, and we are left constantly dissatisfied with our achievements. Often, in stressful situations, the part of us that manifests is an Inner Child part.

To counteract this tendency, we must change how we talk to ourselves. Practising self-compassion does not mean absolving ourselves of responsibility for our actions but treating ourselves with the same understanding and kindness we would treat someone else in the same situation. It means acknowledging that failure and mistakes are part of the shared human experience and that these moments offer valuable opportunities for learning and growth.

Essentially, learning to treat ourselves with more kindness is a process that requires time, patience, and practice. Changing the negative internal dialogue to one that is encouraging and supportive can significantly transform how we face and navigate difficulties, leading to a healthier relationship with ourselves and the world around us.

I invite you to reflect: When going through a difficult situation, we often tend to be very harsh on ourselves, treating ourselves like demanding parents.

- ✓ If you were faced with a child having trouble, feeling vulnerable, or angry, what would you do to help them?

- ✓ How would you assist them in fulfilling their needs?

- ✓ Putting this into perspective is extremely useful for that inner child who often needs more kindness and understanding. Otherwise, we are just like those who abused us in childhood with criticism and perfectionism.

- ✓ What would you say to a vulnerable or angry child in this situation?

Be yourself in your way, Strong, Bold, Inspired

Be yourself in your way

If I don't see you, you don't exist!

"Make your inner world beautiful, and with time, it will reflect in the exterior." -
Eckhart Tolle

Each of us carries within ourselves certain aspects, traits, or memories that we consider less pleasant or even unacceptable, either due to our own personal standards or due to the expectations we perceive from those around us. These parts of the self, which we judge as unwanted or harmful, can induce profound feelings of shame, fear of judgment, and the sense that we are not good enough. To avoid these painful emotions, we often adopt the strategy of avoidance: we refuse to confront these parts, to analyse them, or to accept them as part of ourselves.

The foundation of this avoidance behaviour lies in the human desire to maintain a positive self-image and avoid emotional pain. Shame is a profound emotion that can make us feel exposed and vulnerable to our own criticism or the criticism of others. The feeling of inadequacy or not being enough" can fuel deep fears of rejection or social isolation.

However, over time, this avoidance strategy can have counterproductive effects. Firstly, it limits our capacity for self-awareness and personal growth. The parts of ourselves that we avoid may contain wisdom and valuable lessons about who we are and how we relate to the world. Denying them means missing out on the opportunity to develop ourselves fully and authentically.

Moreover, avoidance maintains and even amplifies the power of unpleasant emotions associated with those aspects of the self. Shame and feelings of inadequacy do not disappear through denial; they can become more acute when left unexamined and ununderstood. This cycle of avoidance and emotional discomfort can also contribute to the development of a negative self-image and disruptions in emotional and psychological well-being.

The key to overcoming this cycle is the courage to confront the parts of ourselves that we have preferred to avoid. This does not mean a process of self-flagellation or harsh self-criticism but rather one of exploration with compassion and understanding. Recognizing and accepting aspects of the self-considered undesirable can be facilitated through practices such as mindfulness, journaling, psychological therapy, or even open and honest conversations with trusted individuals.

Fully accepting ourselves—with our strengths and weaknesses—is not a process that happens overnight. It is a journey of self-discovery and personal growth that requires patience, courage, and, most importantly, compassion. Through acceptance, we give ourselves the opportunity to heal from the burden of shame and feelings of inadequacy and open ourselves up to a more authentic and fulfilling life.

I invite you to reflect: We often avoid the aspects of ourselves that we cannot accept. We avoid focusing on them to avoid feeling the unpleasant emotions of shame and inadequacy. We need to begin focusing on these aspects getting acquainted with them and accepting them.

- ✓ What aspect of yourself can't you truly accept?

Be yourself in your way, Strong, Bold, Inspired

What can you learn from this mistake?

> *"A person who has never made a mistake*
> *has never tried anything new."*
> Albert Einstein

Mistakes are an integral part of the human condition; they are part of the process of learning and personal development. No matter how cautious or attentive we may be, errors in judgment and wrong actions are inevitable. Such moments can bring feelings of guilt, frustration, and self-criticism, leading us into a negative cycle of thoughts and emotions that, far from helping us, can hinder our growth.

A common response to mistakes is self-blame and criticism. This approach often results from very high internal standards and pressure we impose on ourselves to be "perfect." However, excessive self-criticism can lead to decreased self-confidence and avoidance of taking risks or trying new things out of fear of making mistakes again.

In contrast, a more constructive approach is to view mistakes as opportunities for learning. When we realize we have made a mistake, we can interrupt the cycle of self-criticism and ask ourselves, "What can this experience teach me?"

This question encourages us to turn a potentially negative moment into one from which we can extract valuable lessons.

Exploring the experience with curiosity and openness means evaluating the situation objectively without letting negative emotions take control. By asking ourselves what we can learn, we shift our focus from feelings of guilt and shame to a constructive analysis of the situation. Perhaps the mistake has shown us that we need to improve specific skills or that we need to pay more attention to details. Maybe it has taught us to ask for help when facing a challenge, or it has shown us the importance of pausing and reflecting before making important decisions.

The ability to view mistakes as opportunities for growth can help us develop resilience and adaptability. Instead of being overwhelmed by negative feelings, we become better equipped to face challenges and more prepared to take advantage of life's lessons. In this way, we cultivate a growth mindset, which sees us capable of learning from mistakes, surpassing our current limitations, and constantly evolving.

Ultimately, this process of reflection and learning helps us improve our skills and navigate life more efficiently and contributes to developing compassion towards ourselves. By learning to treat ourselves with kindness and understanding in moments of failure, we cultivate a healthier and more positive relationship with ourselves, one based on acceptance and growth rather than self-criticism and blame.

I invite you to reflect: We always make mistakes, and we can't avoid them; despite all precautions, we make errors in judgment. When we realise, we can blame ourselves, criticise ourselves, and feel guilty, or we can stop and listen to that experience:

- ✓ What can it teach us now?
- ✓ How can it be useful to us in the future?

Be yourself in your way, Strong, Bold, Inspired

What would I do if I had more time available?

> *" Time is the currency of your life. It is the only currency you have, and only you can determine how it will be spent. Be careful, or others will spend it for you."*
> Carl Sandburg

The concept of time and how we manage it is deeply reflected in the quality of our lives. Often, we feel like time is our enemy and that we don't have enough of it to accomplish all that we set out to do. This perception of "lack of time" becomes a convenient excuse, an alibi that allows us to procrastinate or even neglect important aspects of our lives that require attention, effort, and, above all, commitment.

Using lack of time as a pretext to avoid doing important things for ourselves can conceal a variety of fears and insecurities. Perhaps we fear the possibility of failure or judgment from others. Maybe we struggle with a lack of clarity regarding what we truly want from life or how to prioritise those things that are truly meaningful to us. Or, perhaps, we avoid confronting our own emotions and deep needs, finding in "lack of time" a convenient shield to hide our vulnerabilities.

If we manage our time efficiently, we often have enough time to make significant progress in the directions that truly matter to us. This requires an honest self-assessment of how we use our time and introspective reflection on the reasons behind our procrastination.

By sincerely asking ourselves what we truly need or want, we can discover what motivates us and what values guide our lives. Clarity helps us identify what is truly important and allocate time for those activities, relationships, or goals that bring us satisfaction, growth, and fulfilment. To achieve this, it's essential to learn to say "no" to demands and distractions that don't serve our objectives and "yes" to those that propel us forward on personal and professional paths.

Setting clear priorities, conscious planning, and practising self-discipline are the foundations of effective time management. However, it's equally important to recognize and allow space for flexibility and rest, acknowledging that efficiency doesn't just mean productivity but also maintaining a healthy balance between work, relaxation, and self-care.

So, overcoming the pretext of lack of time requires sincere introspection and the willingness to confront our avoidance and excuses. By cultivating a more authentic and responsible relationship with our time, we can begin to make more aligned choices with who we are and what we truly want to achieve in life. This process frees us from the false burden of "lack of time" and gives us the chance to live a more fulfilling and balanced life.

I invite you to reflect: We always wish we had more time and we often use this lack as an excuse not to do important things for ourselves, so we don't ask ourselves what we really need.

- ✓ Now, pause for a moment and ask yourself:

- ✓ If I had an extra "slice" of time, what would I do for myself?

- ✓ What would I do if I had more time available?

Be yourself in your way, Strong, Bold, Inspired

Learn to master control!

"We cannot control the wind, but we can adjust the sails."
Seneca

Recognizing the difference between what we can and cannot control in our lives is a fundamental distinction that can free us from the unnecessary burden of anxiety, guilt, and helplessness. Many of the challenges we face daily will be outside our direct sphere of influence, and while this can be frustrating, accepting this fact can pave the way to greater inner peace and resilience.

The aspects of life we can control are often directly related to our actions, thoughts, and behaviours. This includes our attitude toward the situations we face, our emotional reactions, and the decisions we make each day. In contrast, external factors such as other people's actions, unexpected events, or the global economic and social context are largely beyond our control.

The ability to observe and accept this difference is crucial. A pragmatic way to do this is by applying the "Serenity Prayer," which urges us to seek „the serenity to accept the things we cannot change, the courage to change the things we can, and the wisdom to know the difference." Identifying and focusing on the aspects we can influence can enhance our sense of personal efficacy and reduce the feeling of being overwhelmed by circumstances.

When we face a situation we cannot change, changing our attitude toward it can profoundly impact our experience. This process begins with acceptance—acknowledging that certain things are as they are, and that resistance may only add to our suffering. Therefore, instead of fighting against reality, we can seek its positive aspects or the lessons that can be learned.

For example, in the face of failure, instead of losing ourselves in self-blame or frustration over circumstances beyond our control, we can ask ourselves," What can this failure teach me?". This shift in perspective can help us see failure as an opportunity for growth rather than a dead end.

Learning to distinguish between what is and isn't within our control and adjusting our attitudes and responses accordingly can significantly reduce anxiety and feelings of guilt or helplessness. Through acceptance and adaptability, we can find peace in chaos and strength in vulnerability, learning to navigate life with greater grace and resilience.

I invite you to reflect: There are things we can control because they depend on us and things we cannot influence. After all, they do not depend on us.

- ✓ Learning to observe this difference can help us avoid feeling overwhelmed by anxiety, guilt, or helplessness. If we cannot change the situation, we can change our attitude toward the experience:

- ✓ How can we accept that there are things we cannot change?

- ✓ How can we live with imperfection and the feeling of limitation?

Be yourself in your way, Strong, Bold, Inspired

How limited is your comfort zone?

> *" Not lack of power, nor lack of knowledge, but rather lack of will, generates resistance to change."*
> *Vince Lombardi*

Resistance to change is a common human trait. We cling to the familiar, the known, and the safe because they give us a sense of control and comfort. It's natural to have reservations about exploring the unknown, as the fear of failure, judgment from others, or even simple anxiety about the new can be intimidating.

However, embracing change and uncertainty can be a powerful catalyst for personal growth and self-discovery.

Once we step beyond the confines of our comfort zone, we allow ourselves to experience and explore new possibilities. This attempt to do something we've never done before compels us to mobilise resources and perhaps untapped capacities. It's an act of courage that opens the door to new perspectives and new ways of perceiving ourselves.

For example, someone who has long considered taking singing lessons but fears potential criticism or a lack of talent chooses not to pursue their desire. One day, however, they decide to leap, discovering a new and exciting hobby and an unforeseen reservoir of courage and persistence in the face of difficulties. Through this experience, the person begins to see themselves in a different light, not just as someone with a particular set of skills or interests, but as an individual capable of learning, adapting, and growing.

Additionally, change and trying new experiences can help us learn more about what we truly enjoy and what defines us. They allow us to redefine and expand the boundaries of the self. Furthermore, they improve our ability to cope with changes and help us become more flexible and open in our daily lives.

Expanding our horizons and embracing new things can transform our perception of ourselves and the world around us. We discover that we are more than our limited set of experiences and competencies and that our growth potential is nearly limitless. These revelations enrich our lives and encourage us to explore even further, continuously opening ourselves to new experiences and aspects of our own personalities. By doing something we've never done before, we add a new story to our collection of experiences and broaden our self-understanding, making room for a more complex and fulfilled version of ourselves.

I invite you to reflect: We often engage in the same familiar activities, hesitating to change because we believe that certain choices and experiences don't fit our idea of ourselves. But that's not true: sometimes, by doing something we've never done, we discover new experiences, but more importantly, we begin to uncover new aspects of ourselves.

- ✓ What new thing, something I've never done before, can I start experimenting with today?

Be yourself in your way,
Strong, Bold, Inspired

What can I be thankful for today?

"Gratitude doesn't change the scenery. What gratitude does is change our focus on reality."

Robert Holden

ONCE UPON A TIME, there was a bird that lived in the desert, very sick, without feathers, without anything to feed on, without a drop of water to quench its thirst, without a place to shelter from the scorching heat, cursing its life day and night.

One day, an angel crosses that desert, and the bird stops him and asks:

- Where are you going?

- I'm going to a meeting with God, he replies.

Then, the bird asks him to ask God when its suffering will end.

- Of course, I will ask Him, assures the Angel!

Then he bids farewell.

At the meeting with God, the Angel conveys the bird's message.

He tells about its wretched state and asks when that harsh suffering for the frail being will end.

- As long as it has left to live, the bird will not have happiness, says God...

- When the bird hears this, it will be discouraged altogether. Can you suggest a solution for that, though, asks the Angel.

God replies:

- Tell it to repeat, as a sacred prayer, again and again, and again, until the words learn to come out on their own:

"Thank you, Lord, for everything!"

The angel returns to the bird and delivers God's message.

A week later, the angel descends the same path again, encounters the bird once more, and sees it very happy.

Its body was covered with feathers, a small lake appeared nearby, and a plant grew on the shore while the bird sang and danced joyfully.

The angel was amazed at what he saw. He remembered what God had told him—that the bird would not be happy for the remaining time it had left to live.

And yet, gratitude changed everything.

****

The feeling of gratitude is one of the most powerful forces influencing our well-being and perception of life. We celebrate the blessings in our lives through gratitude and amplify our ability to view the world through a more positive and hopeful lens. It is well known that gratitude brings multiple psychological and physical benefits, transforming how we live and interact with the surrounding world.

At a psychological level, practising gratitude helps us counteract the human tendency to focus on negative aspects, difficulties, or what we lack. Acknowledging and appreciating what we have can significantly reduce stress and anxiety, creating space for happiness and satisfaction. Studies suggest that individuals who regularly practice gratitude report lower levels of depression and greater resilience in adversity. This is partly due to gratitude's resetting effect on our emotional system, reminding us of the positive things in our lives and helping us maintain a balanced and optimistic perspective.

In addition to psychological benefits, gratitude has been associated with a range of physical improvements, including better sleep quality, increased resistance to illness, and faster recovery after medical interventions or injuries. Cultivating gratitude can also enhance our interpersonal relationships. By expressing appreciation for the actions of those around us, we build stronger and more authentic connections, creating an environment based on mutual respect and understanding.

Practising gratitude can be simple and inexpensive. It can start with a daily habit of noting three things we are grateful for daily, expressing thanks to those around us for their gestures, or even quietly reflecting on aspects of our lives that bring us joy and fulfilment. Through these seemingly small gestures, gratitude can radically transform our personal experience and how we interact with the world.

In conclusion, gratitude's power lies in transforming our perception of life, opening our hearts to joy, peace, and deep connection with those around us. It is a powerful tool for healing and personal growth, available to anyone willing to direct their attention and appreciation toward the beauty and richness of our everyday existence.

I invite you to reflect. Stop and observe your day, the people around you, the strangers you encounter, and your experiences: there is always something to be grateful for.

Directing our attention to these things, without taking them for granted, makes us happier, more aware of what we have, and more open to others.

Be yourself in your way, Strong, Bold, Inspired

Be yourself in your way

What makes you feel alive?

" Enthusiasm is the fuel of life. Without it, no significant project can be brought to completion."

Dale Carnegie

The things that excite us and spark our eyes are trustworthy sources of energy and inspiration in our lives. These activities, interests, or passions enrich our existence, fill us with joy, and provide us with a profound sense of fulfilment. However, in the hustle and bustle of daily life and under the pressure of obligations and responsibilities, we often give them too little time or prioritise other aspects that seem more urgent or important to us. This is a paradox of the modern human condition: we ignore or postpone exactly those elements that could make our lives more beautiful and meaningful.

The power of activities that excite us lies in their unique ability to reconnect us with our authentic essence. They remind us of who we are when we remove the masks we wear in different social roles. Whether it's painting, music, dance, nature walks, writing, or anything else that truly makes us happy, these activities serve as channels for personal expression and connection to our inner source of creativity and passion.

Moreover, activities that make our eyes sparkle energize us and provide us with the strength to face life's challenges. They can function as a sort of emotional and mental reset, giving us the feeling that we can confidently tackle any difficult situation. Additionally, these passions expand our horizons, enrich our knowledge, and enhance our human qualities, such as empathy, patience, or perseverance.

Despite these undeniable benefits, we often find ourselves trapped in a vicious cycle of „I have to do" instead of making time for „I would like to do." This happens because society values productivity and material success over happiness and personal fulfilment. We prioritise our careers, financial goals, or meeting the expectations of others while neglecting our own emotional and spiritual needs.

Recognising the value and power of exciting activities invites us to reevaluate priorities and make conscious choices that reflect what truly defines and enriches our lives. It is essential to remind ourselves that life is more than just a series of tasks to check off a list; it is a journey filled with moments worth experiencing with passion and enthusiasm.

By choosing to prioritize activities that fill us with positive energy and joy, we not only improve our quality of life but also become a source of inspiration for those around us. By living passionately and finding joy in the little things, we show others that living a meaningful and fulfilling life is possible.

I invite you to reflect. If you've forgotten or are overwhelmed by routine duties, stop and focus on what excites you. Then, make time to nurture this aspect of yourself: We emotionally recharge from our passions and the things we strongly believe in.

What idea, subject, or activity makes you feel alive and makes your eyes sparkle?

Be yourself in your way, Strong, Bold, Inspired

Did I celebrate myself?

> *"Never forget to celebrate the small victories of everyday life, because they contribute to achieving great successes."* –
> Denise Pappas

The tendency to minimize or even ignore our personal achievements is surprisingly common, even among those with undeniable success and accomplishments. This phenomenon can be fuelled by various causes, including high personal standards, comparisons with others, imposter syndrome, or even education excessively emphasising modesty and self-criticism. Regardless of its source, the impact of this tendency is clear: it deprives us of recognising and celebrating our progress, which is essential for maintaining motivation and a positive self-image.

Minimising achievements limits our ability to savour moments of success and can also negatively impact self-esteem and confidence in our abilities. Instead of seeing ourselves as capable individuals, we risk doubting our worth and contributions. This cycle of self-doubt and self-criticism can hinder taking on new challenges and experiencing personal and professional growth.

Rewarding or acknowledging achieved goals is fundamental to encouraging a virtuous circle of self-confidence and healthy ambition. Small rewards or gestures of self-appreciation for our accomplishments, no matter how small they may seem, can help us create a sense of progress and maintain our commitment to long-term goals. These gestures allow us to connect with the feeling of success and fulfilment, essential for sustainable well-being.

Moreover, recognizing and rewarding personal successes can improve our ability to withstand failures and disappointments. By celebrating progress, we remind ourselves that we are in a process of learning and development, where mistakes and failures are natural and necessary steps. This mindset can make us more resilient and more willing to tackle new challenges, knowing that each experience, good or bad, contributes to our growth.

Practically, rewarding achieved goals can take various forms, from a well-deserved break to purchasing a desired item or simply spending quality time with loved ones. What's important is that this recognition is conscious and intentional, a moment where we honour our hard work, dedication, and progress.

In conclusion, turning the recognition and reward of our achievements into a habit can open the door to greater personal satisfaction, self-confidence, and motivation. By celebrating each step forward, no matter how small, we cultivate an attitude of gratitude and appreciation for our unique journey, significantly contributing to personal well-being and happiness.

I invite you to reflect: Is it okay to strive to achieve your goals, but do you stop to celebrate? Do you rejoice in what you have accomplished or is there always something missing to be content with yourself?

- ✓ What is it like to pause and rejoice in your accomplishments?
- ✓ What is your relationship with appreciation and celebration?
- ✓ What achievements or goals bring me joy? Have I celebrated them?

Be yourself in your way, Strong, Bold, Inspired

How could I slow down a bit?

> *" The true power lies within the present moment. The past is a memory. The future, an anticipation. Only the present is real and accessible. Be fully present, and the world will unfold beneath your feet."*
>
> Eckhart Tolle

In the frenetic rhythm of modern life, we often rush from one task to another, from one commitment to the next, seeking to juggle multiple responsibilities and objectives. This continuous race against time can lead us to lose sight of the essential aspects of life, including our well-being, emotions, and authentic human connections. When we live in this state of perpetual hurry, we neglect the signals our body sends us and lose touch with our essence and those around us.

Our bodies are endowed with their wisdom, continuously sending us signals about their needs and limits. Prolonged stress, fatigue, muscle tension, or even emotional disturbances are ways in which the body tries to communicate that it has reached its limits and that it is time to take a break. Ignoring these signals in favour of maintaining a fast pace can lead to physical and emotional exhaustion, ultimately affecting all aspects of our lives.

Furthermore, in the turmoil of tasks and obligations, we tend to disconnect from our emotions and inner experiences, losing access to a vital part of the human experience. This disconnection can be detrimental to ourselves and our relationships with others, as empathy, understanding, and authentic presence in our interactions become compromised.

Slowing down the pace, even for a few minutes a day, can profoundly impact our physical and emotional health. This process of slowing down allows us to take an inner inventory, observe what is happening within us and around us, breathe consciously, and listen to our bodies and emotions. It is a moment where we allow ourselves to simply be present, without doing, without judging, without rushing to the next activity.

This practice of presence and self-awareness can also extend to our relationships. When we take the time to truly listen, observe and appreciate the moments spent with others, our relationships deepen and become more meaningful. We learn to value our loved ones for who they are, not just for the roles they play in our lives.

Therefore, slowing down is more than just a well-deserved break; it's an opportunity to realign with our essential values, needs, and aspirations. It allows us to nurture and nourish our spirit, body, and relationships, rediscovering the joy and profound fulfilment that comes from simply being present in the current moment. Thus, slowing down becomes a form of resistance against external pressures and a path to a more balanced, fulfilling, and connected life.

I invite you to reflect: When we rush, we neglect what we feel, the signals from our bodies, and the opportunity to stay in touch with ourselves and others. We can reconnect with ourselves when we slow down even a little and consistently give ourselves the chance to do so, even for a few minutes.

How could I slow down a bit?

Be yourself in your way, Strong, Bold, Inspired

Make heaven out of what you have: your resources!

" When we can no longer change a situation, we are challenged to change ourselves."
Viktor E. Frankl

The coping mechanisms each of us adopts in the face of stress are essential survival strategies. They allow us to navigate life's challenges, providing temporary means of adapting to pressure and difficulties. Although these mechanisms can vary significantly from person to person, we can generally divide them into three main categories: fight (gritting our teeth and resorting to verbal and physical attack), flight (removing ourselves or avoiding the problem), and freeze or numbness (emotionally detaching from the situation).

When it comes to the flight mechanism, we mobilize both internal and external resources to confront the challenge directly. This coping mechanism can be highly effective in the short term, enhancing our ability to solve problems and face difficulties. However, excessive or exclusive use of this mechanism, especially without adequate support, can lead to mental and physical exhaustion. It's important to remember that while resilience and determination are valuable qualities, recognising limits and seeking help when necessary is equally important for maintaining our mental and physical well-being.

Avoidance or distancing oneself from the problem may seem attractive, especially when the situation appears overwhelming or unbearable. This involves physical or emotional withdrawal, attempting to shield ourselves from immediate discomfort. While it may provide temporary relief, avoidance does not address the underlying issue and, in the long run, can reinforce feelings of helplessness or anxiety. Additionally, it may lead to missed opportunities for personal growth and the accumulation of unresolved problems.

Emotional numbing or detachment from a stressful situation is an attempt to shield ourselves from intense emotional pain or discomfort. Essentially, we "freeze" our emotional responses, maintaining outward calmness while experiencing a whirlwind of unexpressed emotions internally. Emotional numbing is often achieved using substances or habits that are harmful in the long run: overeating, drinking, gambling, social media, pornography, etc.

Although this mechanism can serve as a temporary shield against pain, its prolonged use can distance us from the authentic experience of our emotions, affecting our ability to form deep emotional connections with ourselves and others.

Recognition and understanding of the coping mechanisms we use regarding stress are essential for developing healthier and more sustainable adaptation strategies. It's important to remember that while these automatic strategies may offer temporary relief, taking a proactive approach to challenges, practising self-care, seeking emotional and professional support, and developing a diverse set of coping mechanisms are important for our emotional well-being.

I invite you to reflect: Each of us activates automatic mechanisms to cope with stress: some grit their teeth and push through it; others flee, meaning they distance themselves from the problem; and still others numb themselves, meaning they emotionally detach from the situation.

There is no right or wrong way in emergencies; all are useful precisely because they are automatic mechanisms. But now, stop and think:

- ✓ What strategy do I use most frequently?
- ✓ Is this the most useful one when there is no imminent danger?
- ✓ What aspects of my character are most useful for coping?
- ✓ What are my internal resources, and how can I use them

effectively?

What makes me happy and fulfilled?

> *" Being honest with oneself, despite the entire world, is a greatness that cannot be overshadowed by any external success."*
> Ralph Waldo Emerson

Letting go of aspects or things in our lives can often be necessary for growth or change. Sometimes, it's about letting go of a toxic relationship, harmful habits, or even a job that no longer meets our emotional or professional needs. These releases can be painful initially, but ultimately, they create space for new opportunities and positive experiences. However, when we give up things that are deeply tied to our personal values—such as integrity, love, passion, or commitment to a cause—the price we pay is much higher than mere temporary discomfort.

Letting go of these core values deprives us of the essence that defines us as individuals. What makes us unique and guides our decisions and actions are precisely these values. (Of course, you should know your personal values!). Without them, we lose our direction and purpose, ending up feeling uprooted and meaningless. This sense of loss and uncertainty leads us into constant dissatisfaction and unhappiness because our life no longer resonates with what is truly important to us. Instead of enjoying authenticity and fulfilment, we struggle in a world that no longer feels like it belongs to us.

Moreover, letting go of these values affects our relationships. When not aligned with our values, it isn't easy to cultivate authentic connections with others. The lack of authenticity becomes a barrier between us and those around us, preventing the development of fulfilling and meaningful relationships. This can lead to isolation and loneliness, amplifying feelings of dissatisfaction and unhappiness.

Ultimately, the power to live a life aligned with our personal values is fundamental to feeling fulfilled and happy. This does not mean the path will be free of difficulties. The greatest challenge is often to identify and keep these values at the centre of our existence despite external pressures and temptations. However, the effort to live authentically, following what is most dear to us, is the only way to achieve profound and lasting satisfaction. The challenge thus becomes an opportunity to constantly rediscover and reaffirm us, to grow and evolve in a way that reflects our inner reality and core values.

I invite you to reflect: We can let go of many things in our lives, but if we give up things that are very important to us, tied to certain core values, we pay a very high price: we remain perpetually dissatisfied and unhappy.

- ✓ Do you know what truly makes you happy and fulfilled?
- ✓ What are the experiences that make you happy and fulfilled?
- ✓ Why are these experiences important to you?
- ✓ Remember these experiences and make sure they have a special place in your day and in your life.

Be yourself in your way, Strong, Bold, Inspired

What is my body telling me?

"Your body is a temple. Listen to it and discover the secrets to a healthy and harmonious life."

Eckhart Tolle

The human body is a complex and sophisticated system, both biologically, emotionally, and psychologically. In many ways, it is our primary communication with the world and ourselves. Without uttering a single word, our body can convey a wide range of emotions and inner states—from joy and relaxation to stress and anxiety. Often, the body reacts to emotional or psychological states even before our mind is fully aware of them, sending us physical signals that can be interpreted as clues to our internal state.

For example, the sensation of "butterflies" in the stomach before an important presentation, the tension in the shoulders and neck after a stressful day, or the pleasant feeling of warmth and relaxation after a happy experience. These somatic reactions are valuable clues that can help us recognize and better understand what we are feeling.

The ability to listen to our body and interpret its signals requires practice and conscious presence. Techniques such as mindfulness or yoga can train our minds to be more attentive to the subtleties of our bodies. This process helps us establish a deeper and more understanding connection with ourselves, providing us with a powerful tool for self-regulation and emotional management.

As we become more attentive to the messages of our body, we notice not only how it reacts to stress or joy but also the factors that trigger these states. This can help us identify aspects of our lives that may require adjustments—whether it's relationships, work, or even personal habits. A body that is frequently tense and exhausted may signal the need for rest and recovery, while persistent feelings of restlessness or agitation may indicate the need for more profound changes in our lives or in our way of thinking.

In a world that often encourages us to prioritise the mind and reason, reconnecting with our body and learning the language of our body—listening to its somatic signals—represents an essential step in developing a healthy emotional and psychological balance. The body thus becomes a valuable ally in our journey towards well-being and self-awareness, helping us better understand our needs and navigate with greater wisdom through the complexities of life.

I invite you to reflect. Our body tells us a lot about what we feel, even before we find the right words to describe our physical sensations or thoughts.

If we learn to listen to our body and train ourselves to do so, we begin to better understand ourselves and our needs.

Start practising what we call "body scan" or yoga Nidra daily. On YouTube, you can find audio dedicated to the practice. If you're not used to it, it might initially seem difficult but start experimenting anyway.

Be yourself in your way, Strong, Bold, Inspired

What is my relationship with my energies?

" To take good care of others, you must first take good care of yourself."

Audrey Hepburn

Our relationship with our energy and how we manage our effort and resources are indicators of our physical health and emotional and psychological well-being. This relationship deeply reflects how we value ourselves and respect our boundaries and needs.

For some, the tendency to constantly strive can manifest as a desire to prove their worth to others or even to themselves. This way of being can lead to exhaustion, chronic stress, and, ultimately, a decrease in performance and personal satisfaction. In this scenario, the relationship with one's energy is often based on pushing through and neglecting the body's warning signals, which can negatively affect our long-term well-being.

On the other hand, there is also a tendency to give up too easily when faced with challenges or discomfort. This can indicate a lack of confidence in our own abilities and resources, as well as a need to avoid difficulties or failures. In these cases, the relationship with our energy is marked by avoidance and underutilization, limiting opportunities for growth and personal development.

A balance in this relationship occurs when we learn to listen to and respect our own body and emotional signals, understanding moment by moment what we can do and how to adjust our efforts. This commitment to being present and receptive to our own needs allows us to manage our energy in a healthier and more sustainable way. It enables us to set healthy boundaries for ourselves, to recognize when we need rest, and when we can push our limits a little further.

Active internal listening and self-observation help us recognize and navigate fluctuations in our energy levels. Through this process, we learn the importance of pauses and rest and how to use moments of increased energy to pursue our passions and achieve our goals. It also becomes possible to identify sources of energy in our lives—activities, relationships, and habits that fuel and revitalize us.

Therefore, the relationship with our own energy is a barometer of how we relate to our own needs and limits. Having a healthy relationship with our energy means respecting and taking care of ourselves physically and cultivating emotional resilience and growing in wisdom and self-sufficiency. Through this carefully cultivated relationship, we become better at managing life's challenges, more confident in our ability to face the unknown, and ultimately more fulfilled in our personal journey.

I invite you to reflect:

- ✓ The way we relate to effort and our resources says a lot about the quality of the relationship we have with ourselves.
- ✓ Do I tend to strive too much?
- ✓ Do I give up too quickly?
- ✓ Do I commit to listening to myself to understand moment by moment what I can do?
- ✓ Do I tend to strive, give up, or listen to my energy level to calibrate it?

Try to pay attention to this.

Be yourself in your way, Strong, Bold, Inspired

The Free Inner Child

" Children do not give up toys because they have grown old; they grow old because they have given up toys."
C.S. Lewis

Deep within each of us lies a profound and essential layer of our being, that aspect of the self which remains eternally youthful, spontaneous, and full of curiosity: our childlike part. This part embodies our ability to marvel, to explore freely without prejudice, and to experience pure joy in life's simple moments. Even as maturity and responsibilities shape us as we age, our emotional health and overall well-being are deeply connected to accessing this inner part and expressing it in our daily lives.

Nurturing our childlike aspect doesn't mean living in denial of our responsibilities or making reckless choices. Instead, it involves allowing ourselves moments of relaxation, risking trying new activities without fear of failure, and rediscovering the sources of joy and enthusiasm that fill our hearts. It's about setting aside internal criticism and building a safe space for the expression of our authentic selves, where creativity and imagination can flourish without constraints.

Nurturing this part can take various forms for each person. It might mean engaging in creative activities like drawing, painting, or writing, which allow for free expression and exploration without the fear of judgment. For others, it might mean rediscovering the pleasure in childhood games, whether it's sports, board games, or simply the joy of swinging on a swing in the park or being in contact with nature.

Moreover, it brings benefits to allow ourselves to experience the world with the same innocent curiosity we had as children. This may mean allowing ourselves to be surprised and amazed by the beauty and mystery of nature, to learn something new with enthusiasm, or simply to truly laugh, from the bottom of our hearts, at the little things.

The quality of our relationship with ourselves is profoundly enhanced when we allow ourselves to nourish and care for this Inner Child. It enables us to establish a deeper connection with our authentic selves, contributing to an overall state of well-being. This helps us maintain mental flexibility, regain our resilience in the face of challenges, and enhance our capacity for empathy and forming authentic connections with others. Essentially, taking care of our Inner Child reminds us that, regardless of age or responsibilities, life remains an adventure worthy of being lived with enthusiasm and openness.

I invite you to reflect: To be well, we must take care of and nurture our Inner Child.

- ✓ How much space is there in your life to play, have fun, feel pleasure, and laugh out loud?
- ✓ How can I nourish the playful and free part of myself?

Be yourself in your way, Strong, Bold, Inspired

If I had to tell a five-year-old, how would I say it?

> *" The first rule of effective communication is to know what you want to say".*
> Sigmund Freud

In the complexity of the adult world, communication can often get lost in a maze of unclear words, jargon, and indirect formulations. Whether expressing personal needs, setting clear boundaries, or even sharing aspects about oneself, dialogue can become so laden with nuances that the initial message becomes diluted or lost altogether. This ambiguous communication style hinders mutual understanding and leaves us feeling like we haven't been fully heard or understood.

Returning to a more straightforward and more direct form of expression can be particularly effective in clarifying and conveying our ideas. Here, interacting with children or imagining how we would communicate a specific concept to a 5-year-old becomes extremely valuable. Children of this age are in a phase where honesty and simplicity are essential; they prefer and best understand clear and direct language devoid of ambiguity.

When we struggle to express our needs or feelings, asking ourselves, "How would I explain this to a 5-year-old?" can help us get back to the essentials. This approach forces us to overcome unnecessary complications and identify the core of what we genuinely want to say. We need to find the most straightforward and direct formulation, eliminate technical terms or ambiguities, and focus on our message's essence.

The strategy of simplifying and clarifying our messages by thinking about how we would communicate them to a child improves the quality of communication in adult relationships and helps us connect more deeply with ourselves. Often, in trying to find the right words to explain a concept to a child, we are forced to reflect more deeply on what we truly feel or believe. This can be a powerful practice of self-reflection and internal clarification.

Furthermore, this approach reminds us of the importance of empathy and patience in communication. By understanding the need for simplicity and clarity in expression to be understood by a child, we are more inclined to apply the same principles in everyday interactions.

Communication, in the simplest and most authentic terms, is about dialogue effectiveness, building healthier relationships, and better self-understanding. Drawing inspiration from children's curiosity and simple wisdom, we can discover more precise and meaningful communication pathways.

I invite you to reflect: Many times, when we need to talk about ourselves, when we need to ask for what we need, we spin around in circles, and we drown in words. To get straight to the point and regain some simplicity, think about it and give it a try:

How would you explain it to a 5-year-old?

Be yourself in your way, Strong, Bold, Inspired

What would I want to tell my teenage Self?

> *"We take care of our flowers just like we take care of ourselves: water, sunlight, soil. We develop our gardens and cultivate our soil."*
>
> Maya Angelou

Inner dialogue is essential to the human experience, yet how we address ourselves can profoundly impact our self-esteem and overall well-being. It's surprising how often we treat ourselves harshly, criticizing our actions and decisions with a severity we rarely apply when it comes to others. This self-criticism can demoralise and become a significant obstacle to personal growth and happiness.

An essential aspect in changing this negative inner dialogue is adopting an attitude of compassion and encouragement towards oneself, akin to a loving and understanding parent. A loving and understanding parent doesn't punish their child for mistakes or imperfections but guides them with kindness, acknowledging that mistakes are part of the learning process. Additionally, a loving parent will encourage their child to try again, to learn from experiences, and to grow while providing the necessary emotional support at the same time.

Applying the same approach to ourselves, we should strive to offer support and encouragement instead of harsh criticism. When facing challenges or failures, let's take a step back to gain perspective and address ourselves with kindness and compassion, recognising that every experience, good or bad, is an opportunity for learning. Let's practice self-compassion and acknowledge that being human means being imperfect but that every step, small or large, brings us closer to who we want to be.

Remembering that we need time and patience to grow is also valuable. Just as a parent shows patience and understanding in the face of their child's development, so must we offer ourselves patience and time to evolve, learn, and adapt. Implementing such a positive and encouraging approach in our inner dialogue can transform how we see ourselves and navigate life.

Practising compassion and gentleness towards oneself is an art that requires time and dedication to master. From acknowledging our emotions to providing validation and support for ourselves in difficult moments, this process of self-awareness and self-care can empower us to live more balanced and fulfilling lives.

Essentially, treating ourselves with the same love, patience, and respect as a loving parent transforms our inner dialogue into one that supports personal growth and development, rather than discouraging or hindering us. This is the foundation upon which we can build a healthy self-relationship, thereby improving our quality of life and helping us navigate the world with more confidence and resilience.

I invite you to reflect: We often treat ourselves very harshly when we talk to ourselves. Sometimes, giving good advice takes a little distance from the issues and a bit more experience. Let's treat ourselves as loving and encouraging parents would.

Now think about yourself when you were 15 years old: what did you need to hear to help and encourage you? Can you do that now?

Be yourself in your way, Strong, Bold, Inspired

What do I want to change and why?

> *"Change is the law of life. Those who only look to the past or present will surely miss the future."*
>
> John F. Kennedy

The change of things we don't like in our lives is a universal and profound theme that has captured the attention of philosophers, psychologists, and thinkers. This process involves external aspects of our existence and, more importantly, an inner transformation.

One of the fundamental principles in approaching change is the recognition that our only true control is over our thoughts, emotions, and actions. The Stoic philosopher Epictetus asserted that "it is not events that disturb people, but their judgments about events." Thus, the first step towards change often involves a review of our perceptions and attitudes, which can reveal that some "problems" are, in fact, challenges that offer growth opportunities.

Another important aspect is the power of habits. "We are what we repeatedly do," said Aristotle, emphasising the importance of small daily actions in shaping our lives. Change often requires a profound review of our routines and daily habits, which, although they may seem insignificant now, collectively define the direction of our lives.

Moreover, the change process is deeply intertwined with our ability to cope with failure and disappointment. As J.K. Rowling said in a speech about the benefits of failure, "Failure gave me an inner security that I had never attained by passing examinations." Failure is often a cornerstone for growth, allowing us to learn from mistakes and focus on what truly matters to us..

Change also requires a significant dose of courage and vulnerability. Letting go of the familiar and moving towards the unknown involves a leap of faith and the ability to remain open in uncertainty. Brene Brown, a researcher and author, speaks about the power of vulnerability and how it allows us to live authentic and fulfilled lives.

In the end, change also involves a long-term commitment. As James Clear, the author of "Atomic Habits," says, small and consistent change brings the most profound and lasting transformations in our lives. We can achieve significant long-term changes by focusing on small and steady improvements.

Reflections and theories about change show us that, despite the challenges and unknowns it may bring, it is intrinsic to personal growth and evolution. By accepting that change is an inevitable and necessary part of life, we can embrace our inner strength and steer towards a more prosperous and more fulfilling future.

I invite you to reflect:

- ✓ When you think about yourself and the things you can't accept, what would you like to change?
- ✓ Stop and make a list of the changes you desire.
- ✓ Then ask yourself: why?
- ✓ After the first answer, ask yourself again: why?
- ✓ And then again, why?

Change is lazy and demanding; it always requires deep motivation. And so, you can challenge it.

Be yourself in your way, Strong, Bold, Inspired

Be yourself in your way

What can I do now to become the person I want to be?

"Constantly remind yourself of the brevity of your existence."
Horatius

With every breath you take, you draw closer to the moment of death.

The realization that our lives have an end is one of the most profound insights we can have as human beings. Detaching from the illusion of our eternity can act as a powerful catalyst for change and personal growth. However, many struggle to confront this reality directly, often preferring the comfort provided by the idea that there is still plenty of time ahead. This perception can lead to procrastination, improper prioritisation of personal values, and regret.

Ernest Becker's work, "The Denial of Death", explores the idea that much of human behaviour is an attempt to deny or minimize the awareness of death. Modern society, with its fast pace and emphasis on material achievements, often reinforces this tendency, diverting attention away from reflecting on the finitude of life and its significance.

However, realising that life is of limited duration and acknowledging that each day is precious can fundamentally change how we choose to live. This awareness can encourage us to live more authentically, express our love openly, and pursue what truly impassions us rather than deferring or getting lost in trivialities.

An emphasis on this awareness doesn't mean living in fear of death or feeling overwhelmed by it, but rather embracing life with more courage and meaning. Steve Jobs, in his Stanford commencement speech, spoke about how the awareness of death was one of the most essential tools for making big decisions in life, saying, "Remembering that I'll be dead soon is the most important tool I've ever encountered to help me make the big choices in life."

We can begin to change our perspective by practising gratitude and mindfulness. Appreciating the small joys, valuing relationships, and dedicating time for reflection and meditation can help us live our lives to the fullest.

Also, it's essential to set our priorities based on our authentic values, not on society's or others' expectations. This may mean, for some, travelling more; for others, dedicating themselves to a passion or spending quality time with loved ones.

Ultimately, everyone should confront this question: "If this were my last year of life, would I live differently? How?" The answer to this question can reveal much about what we should change, allowing us to live with a more profound sense of purpose and fulfilment.

I invite you to reflect:

- ✓ If you imagine yourself on the last day of your life, how would you like to be?

- ✓ What changes would you want to have made in your life?

- ✓ Fantasies alone are not enough, so open your eyes and start now: what changes can you start making to move in that direction?

- ✓ And if you start acting now, where do you see yourself in a year? Where do you see yourself in five years?

Be yourself in your way, Strong, Bold, Inspired

Section: Me and Others

What do I see in the eyes of others?

> *" Those who irritate us the most are our most sincere mirrors."*
> C.S. Lewis

Self-image is a highly complex concept, often shaped by the perceptions and feedback we receive from those around us. These social mirrors can significantly influence how we see ourselves and how we evaluate our abilities, character, and even physical appearance. While it's crucial to maintain a certain level of independence and authenticity in our self-perception, we cannot ignore the impact of others' observations on us.

Others can often offer a new, sometimes surprising perspective on us, which can help us discover hidden potentials or identify certain aspects that need improvement. It could be a talent you've never recognized or a habit that holds you back but that you consider harmless.

In this journey of self-exploration and self-definition, a vital first step is to begin listening to and examining the feedback received. However, it's essential to approach this analysis with a balance between open-mindedness and a healthy internal critic. A key question is, „What resonates with me and what doesn't?".

Precisely, you can eliminate misconceptions that don't serve your development and focus on those that truly reflect who you are or who you want to become.

Alongside this internal reflection arises the question: „Is there something more than others don't see in me?". It's possible that specific characteristics or talents may be subdued or unexpressed for various reasons—whether it's due to shyness, fear of judgment, or simply a lack of opportunities to showcase them. Reflecting on this question gives you the chance to rediscover and harness competencies or hidden aspects of your personality.

When considering whether to willingly reveal these hidden aspects, it's essential to ask yourself what your intention is behind this decision. If the purpose is authenticity and the desire to share a more complete version of yourself with others, then it's a step in the right direction. However, if the motives are dictated by societal expectations or the desire to please others, it might be time to reassess the decision.

Developing a positive and realistic self-image is a dynamic process that requires introspection, openness to feedback, and the courage to express oneself authentically. Maintaining a balance between considering others' perspectives and remaining true to your own essence is crucial. This balance will help you navigate life's challenges with a deeper understanding of yourself and an enhanced capacity for adaptation and personal growth.

I invite you to reflect: Our self-image is also influenced by what others say about us. We don't always have the whole truth about ourselves, and often others offer an interesting perspective on us.

Start looking at it. Then, ask yourself: what fits with me and what doesn't?

Finally, is there something about me that others don't see? Am I willingly showing it?

Choose a person from your circle, someone you care about. How does this person see me? If it's not expressed through direct communication, what non-verbal cues are there? How do they see me? How do they perceive me? Sometimes, actions speak louder than words.

Note the discrepancies. Note if you're trying to impress, manipulate, or make them believe something else about you. Observe your communication with this person. Are you able to be sincere and honest? To show yourself as you are, or are you embellishing the image you present? Why?

Envy, bitter fruit

> *" Envy is a waste of time. We focus on what others have, instead of concentrating on what we can achieve ourselves." -*
> *Robert Herjavec*

Envy, often considered a negative emotion, is accompanied by a strong stigma in society. We usually feel a particular shame when we admit to envying someone, as we like to believe that we are above such "inferior" feelings. Despite its bad reputation, envy can serve a constructive purpose and can be transformed into a motivational force for personal growth.

When envy pushes us to recognise the qualities or successes we admire in others, it offers us a mirror to our desires and aspirations. Understanding what triggers our feelings of envy can be extremely enlightening. It helps us identify which values we appreciate most, and which aspects of our lives await improvement or development.

For example, if we envy a colleague's professional success, this feeling may signal a deep longing for recognition in our own career or a burning desire to develop our skills and abilities. In this context, envy doesn't have to be a condemnation but rather an impulse towards action. It can motivate us to set clearer goals, seek new learning and development opportunities, or even start a project we've been putting off.

Transforming envy into a motivating force requires sincerity and introspection. The first step is to accept the feeling without judgment, recognizing it as a useful indicator of our unfulfilled desires. Then, armed with this knowledge, we can direct our energy and resources towards balancing those areas of our lives that make us feel inadequate.

In an ideal world, we could inspire each other without feeling envy.

Until then, we can use this complex feeling as a tool for self-awareness and personal growth, interpreting it as a clear signal that there are aspects of our lives worth exploring and, eventually, transforming. Thus, envy, though challenging to manage, can become an unexpected ally in our journey towards self-improvement and fulfilment.

I invite you to reflect: Envy is an emotion that doesn't have a good reputation: we feel ashamed when we experience it. However, it is useful: it helps us see what we appreciate in others, how we want to become, and what we want to learn.

- ✓ It is helpful to ask ourselves: what can I do to move in that direction?
- ✓ How can I channel my energy and resources to achieve what I desire and envy in others?
- ✓ How can this emotion help me?

Be yourself in your way, Strong, Bold, Inspired

The difference between a plain and a garden

> *" If you want to be respected by others, the most important step is to respect yourself. Show your boundaries clearly." –*
> *Miyamoto Musashi*

It can often happen, whether out of a desire to be agreeable or a fear of rejection, that we behave as if we are a vast, open plain for others. We present ourselves as a territory they can explore without encountering any fences or signs saying, "This far and no further." In this metaphor, we become a space where rules and boundaries are absent, where others feel free to act unrestrained, ignoring our personal needs and limits—either unconsciously or consciously. This behaviour can lead to feelings of unfulfillment, exhaustion, and even a loss of self-respect, as we continually put ourselves last.

Establishing healthy boundaries is essential for harmonious coexistence and mental and emotional well-being. Healthy boundaries define us as individuals and indicate what we consider acceptable or unacceptable in our relationships. They protect our personal space, ensure self-respect, and allow us to maintain our internal balance.

Without these boundaries, relationships can become dysfunctional. It's like allowing the wind to blow in all directions across an unbounded plain, leaving deep and chaotic marks. Without boundaries, we lose our direction and can be easily hurt. On the other hand, communicating our expectations and what we can or cannot tolerate in interactions with others builds symbolic fences that protect both personal integrity and the integrity of relationships.

It is essential to understand that setting boundaries does not mean being rigid or inhospitable. On the contrary, boundaries allow us to maintain healthier and more authentic relationships where communication is open, and each party understands and respects the other's needs. Healthy boundaries allow us to express ourselves in a way that respects ourselves and others while ensuring an environment conducive to mutual growth and respect.

In conclusion, presenting ourselves as an unlimited plan for others may seem like an invitation to freedom and openness, but in the long run, it proves unsustainable and harmful. Recognising and setting healthy boundaries is a sign of deep self-respect and concern for the quality of our relationships. It is an act of balance that protects and defines us, allowing us to navigate human interactions with dignity and harmony.

I invite you to reflect: Sometimes we present ourselves to others as if we were an open plain where they can move freely, without limits, without respecting or applying any rules, without considering the boundaries we deem necessary to feel comfortable with others.

- ✓ It is important to recognize and become aware of these boundaries by others to protect our time, resources, and values.

- ✓ What can I do today to interact with others as if I were a beautiful, lush garden with a gate that I choose to open and close?

- ✓ What boundaries do I need to set between myself and others?

Be yourself in your way, Strong, Bold, Inspired

With whom and what do I need to clarify?

> *" Don't wait for the perfect moment; take the present moment and make it perfect." -*
> *Zoey Sayward*

The burden of unresolved issues feels like a weight on our shoulders, clouding our thoughts and disturbing our inner peace. Whether dealing with minor misunderstandings or significant conflicts, these tend to accumulate within us, creating a heaviness that slows our steps and darkens our perception of life. It is common to feel like prisoners of the past, trapped in a cage of regrets and "what ifs," which prevents us from enjoying the freedom and peace we deeply desire.

Acknowledging that wounds and misunderstandings are an integral part of human relationships' dynamics is essential in this journey toward liberation and reconciliation. We are complex beings with our own aspirations, beliefs, and perceptions, which inevitably can lead to discord and conflict. However, repairing and healing these fractures is possible and essential for personal growth and development.

Authentic and open communication is one of the most powerful tools in repairing ruptures. Honest discussions, where parties express their feelings, fears, and desires without blame or guilt, can lay the groundwork for reconciliation. It is crucial to practice active listening, understand the other person's perspective, and put us in their shoes, even when our emotions are still raw.

Additionally, when discussing repairing ruptures, we must sincerely ask ourselves if we are willing to offer forgiveness and take responsibility for our part. Forgiveness does not mean denying the pain or accepting inappropriate behaviour, but rather releasing the burden of resentment to regain our own inner peace and freedom. Acknowledging our own contribution to the situation, even though passive acceptance of behaviour that hurt us, can be a significant and courageous step towards healing.

In addition to this, it is essential to give ourselves space and time for reflection and healing. Sometimes, resolution may not come immediately, and the reconciliation process can be gradual, requiring patience and perseverance.

In conclusion, the ability to repair ruptures in our relationships not only helps us feel freer and at peace but also transforms us into more mature beings, capable of managing conflict healthily and building bridges of understanding and authentic connection with those around us. It is a journey that requires us to be vulnerable, courageous, and above all, willing to grow and learn from life's experiences.

I invite you to reflect: Sometimes, we carry with us small or big unresolved issues that tire us from within and prevent us from feeling fully free and at peace with our experiences, our choices, and ourselves. It's natural to be hurt or to have misunderstandings in relationships, but what's important is to learn how to repair the ruptures.

- ✓ Ask yourself: With whom do I need to clarify something?

Sometimes it's enough to tell the other person what we felt, how we felt during that experience. Try it.

Be yourself in your way, Strong, Bold, Inspired

The grass, the neighbour's goat, and the wife

" Comparison is the thief of happiness."
Theodore Roosevelt

Most of us become familiar with the game of comparison from a very young age. It is induced in us, sometimes subtly, other times more directly, by the culture of society, by the education we receive, and even by our daily interactions. It's such a common practice that it can become second nature without us always realizing the impact it can have on our well-being and self-respect.

This habit of comparing ourselves to others may seem deceptively harmless or even motivating. After all, it can temporarily function as a lever that propels us towards becoming "better," or it seemingly provides a way to measure our success. However, in the long run, this behaviour fuels an endless chase after the wind, where standards of success and happiness are constantly shifting, always dependent on others.

The main problem with this approach is that it often stems from a place of insecurity and self-criticism. Comparing ourselves to others often means either judging ourselves too harshly or judging others, which interferes with our ability to embrace and appreciate our uniqueness and that of others. Everyone has a unique journey, with their own challenges, victories, and lessons to learn. When we forget to acknowledge this, when we try to measure our worth through the achievements or failures of others, we only undermine our intrinsic value.

So, instead of getting caught up in this perpetuum mobile of endless comparisons, it would be more constructive to channel our energy and attention towards self-appreciation and self-development. This involves recognizing and celebrating our own achievements, embracing our imperfections, and working on them at our own pace, without the pressure of "keeping up" with others.

By learning to value our own journey, we discover the freedom and authentic happiness that are not tied to comparison but to acceptance and personal growth.

In the end, the key is to understand that each of us has a unique value, a story that defines and distinguishes us. Reminding ourselves of this and moving away from the need to compare ourselves to others will allow us to live more meaningful, authentic, and ultimately happier lives. Let's remember that the only person worth comparing ourselves to is our past self, and let's aspire to be a better version today and work towards the version of tomorrow. As a famous advertising slogan goes:" More than yesterday, less than tomorrow!"

I invite you to reflect: We often play the comparison game; we've learned it since we were young. However, now that we've grown up, we must remember that comparing ourselves to others is not very constructive, as it fuels self-criticism or harsh judgment of others. Often, we make these comparisons to feel better about ourselves. Now, stop and observe who you compare yourself to most often:

- ✓ What do I admire about this person?
- ✓ What do I envy?
- ✓ What can I appreciate about myself and the other person?
- ✓ How can I develop in myself what I envy in the other? Am I sure I need it?

Be yourself in your way, Strong, Bold, Inspired

With mask, without mask

> *" People wear masks, and for a good while, you can't know who they are or what they want, until one day they no longer have the energy to hold the mask, and their true face is revealed." – Paulo Coelho*

The masks and roles we adopt in society are often influenced by our need for belonging, acceptance, and appreciation from others. Masks can serve as a means of protection, allowing us to navigate through various social contexts while maintaining a self-image that aligns with external expectations. However, this attitude can be so complex and subtle that we often don't even realise we're wearing a mask.

People may not always be aware of the masks they wear. Some of these roles are so well integrated into our identity that we lose clarity about the boundary between our authentic selves and the characters we play. This often happens because, since childhood, we are taught and shaped by our environment to behave in a certain way to be accepted and loved.

Roles and masks can be useful to some extent. They can help us function in society, providing us with a framework to navigate daily interactions and challenges.

For example, the role of a professional in the workplace requires a certain demeanour and behaviour different from what we might exhibit in an informal context with friends. These roles can simplify the complexity of human relationships and facilitate teamwork, leadership, and other essential social interactions.

Problems arise when these masks prevent us from living authentically and establishing deep human connections. If we wear a mask for too long, we can lose touch with who we are, with our authentic needs, desires, and values. This internal dissonance can lead to stress, anxiety, and other mental health issues.

Masks become harmful when they exhaust us when we feel we must perpetuate a false facade that does not reflect our true selves. If we constantly feel the need to hide or deny our identity to be accepted, we may end up experiencing emotional exhaustion and feeling isolated.

The solution is not necessarily to completely abandon roles or masks, but rather to become more aware of them, to understand why we adopted them and how much they define us. It is vital to seek balance and to have relationships where we can be completely honest and vulnerable without fear of judgment. By accepting our vulnerability and practising authenticity, we can build a life where the roles we play support us rather than burden us. Ultimately, the path to an authentic self is an ongoing project of self-discovery and acceptance, which requires courage and honesty.

I invite you to reflect: How do you describe yourself when you must introduce yourself? Sometimes, we attach a lot of labels that define our roles as parents, spouses, professionals, and so on. This is certainly true and is part of our identity. But if you stop and think about yourself:

- ✓ Who are you to yourself, regardless of all these roles?
- ✓ How would you answer yourself?
- ✓ Who am I when I strip away my roles?

Be yourself in your way, Strong, Bold, Inspired

My sacred space

" Peace comes from within. Don't seek it outside." - Buddha

Solitude, often misunderstood as isolation or loneliness, can be a sacred space for personal growth and self-discovery. In the constant noise of contemporary life, where we are continuously bombarded by external stimuli and find rare moments of pause, solitude offers an oasis of tranquillity and precious time to be with oneself.

However, for many of us, the comfort in chaos and busyness hides a reluctance to confront silence. In silence and deep solitude, the mind begins to speak louder, and the emotions we've pushed into the silent chamber of our hearts begin to erupt. This can be uncharted territory or one we try to avoid out of fear of what we might find there. The discomfort arises because we've become so accustomed to being distracted that we forget how to be present with ourselves.

The fear of solitude and silence often has deep roots in the fear of introspection. Being alone with oneself means being forced to confront one's own thoughts, doubts, fears, unfulfilled aspirations, and unresolved emotions. This process can seem overwhelming, but it's also extremely liberating and healing. When we stop running away from ourselves and embrace our vulnerabilities and imperfections, we experience profound acceptance and inner peace.

Spending time in solitude, deliberately and consciously, can be transformative. We learn to enjoy our own company, cherish moments of silence, and use these moments for reflection and meditation. Solitude allows us to disconnect from external noise to reconnect with ourselves, providing space to listen to what our hearts and soul have to say.

As we become familiar with this practice, we can find calmness even in the whirlwind of daily life. We develop emotional resilience, learn to manage our emotions and thoughts better, and discover a path to authenticity and self-expression.

Thus, solitude should not be seen as a feared enemy but rather as a friend and guide who helps us return to our deepest essence. In chosen silence and loneliness, we learn to love, accept, and heal ourselves, discovering the beauty and power of being present with ourselves.

I invite you to reflect: We must cultivate silence to feel comfortable in our skin and learn to feel good in our own company, even when alone. Sometimes, we feel uncomfortable with silence and avoid it because, in those moments, we can hear our minds speaking and emotions bursting out. And yet, only in those moments, if we don't cover them with anything else, can we listen to ourselves and tune in with ourselves first and then with others.

- ✓ How can I achieve more tranquillity?

Be yourself in your way, Strong, Bold, Inspired

Cast the first stone if you dare!

> *" What you say about others reveals more about you than about them."*
> Eleanor Roosevelt

What bothers us about others can surprisingly serve as a mirror to our being. Often, the behaviours, attitudes, or even personality traits of others that we find annoying or worthy of criticism can reveal hidden or unresolved areas within ourselves. Often unconscious, this phenomenon can offer valuable insights into our personal and emotional development.

Therefore, when we feel the impulse to criticise or try to correct someone, it is worth taking a step back and reflecting on our motives. The tendency to reject certain behaviours in others may signal that the same issues exist or have existed in our lives.

For example, we might be irritated by others' selfishness because, on a deeper level, we struggle with our selfish tendencies or because we have been hurt by someone with such behaviours.

Furthermore, this introspection can reveal that by criticising others, we are, to some extent, trying to distance ourselves from aspects of our personality that we do not want to acknowledge. If I condemn someone else's behaviour, it's because I consider myself immaculate, and I cannot and would never have that behaviour! Thus, we can transform our external frustration into self-awareness and self-improvement by recognising this mechanism.

Furthermore, understanding that many of our frustrations with others reflect our inner state can help us develop empathy and tolerance towards others. This process of awareness can allow us to approach our relationships with more understanding and patience, granting ourselves and others the grace to be imperfect and constantly growing.

The things that annoy us about others can be revealing for our self-understanding. By learning to explore the reasons behind our frustrations and using them as opportunities for introspection and personal growth, we can transform negative experiences into valuable opportunities for spiritual and emotional enrichment.

I invite you to reflect: The things that annoy us about others, the ones we criticise or try to correct, often resonate with something from our history. They are primarily about us. So, next time this happens, stop, and ask yourself:

- ✓ What within me drives me to condemn and criticise the other person?

Be yourself in your way, Strong, Bold, Inspired

How can I make you understand that I love you?

„People feel loved when they perceive that their partner truly appreciates them and validates their needs and desires."
Gary Chapman

The idea that we perceive, and express love differently is not just an observation of our daily experiences but also a crucial foundation in the psychology of interpersonal relationships. In his work "The Five Love Languages," Gary Chapman categorizes these modes of expressing and understanding love into five primary "languages": words of affirmation, quality time, receiving gifts, acts of service, and physical touch. These distinctions help us understand that a profound gesture of love for one person may not hold the same significance for another.

When differences in expressing love are not understood or accepted in a relationship, it can lead to feelings of neglect, unappreciation, or misunderstanding. One partner might believe that dedicating their time and attention is the sincerest form of expressing love, while the other might expect verbal affirmations and appreciation to feel loved.

Therefore, it is essential to recognize and respect your partner's love language and communicate your own love language. This means making a conscious effort to express love in the most easily perceived way by our partner, even if it is not natural for us. For example, if your partner appreciates receiving gifts as proof of love, finding small tokens of affection for them can make a significant difference, even if you do not place much emphasis on gifts.

A significant challenge in this process is developing the ability to identify and understand the other person's love language, which requires empathy, active listening, and openness to exploring the emotional depths of the other person. This endeavour is not limited to romantic relationships but applies to all forms of relationships - from friendships and family to coworkers.

Success in this process requires a continuous commitment from both individuals to ensure that love is not only expressed but also received in a way that meets each person's emotional needs. Developing and improving how we express and perceive love can lead to deeper, more fulfilling relationships.

I invite you to reflect: Each of us understands that we are loved by the other through specific gestures or behaviours. The idea is that often we speak different languages or use different behaviours and ways to express what we feel. Being aware of how we communicate and receive affection can also help us to observe more closely or to ask what ways the other person uses.

- ✓ How do I know that I am loved?
- ✓ Through what gesture or behaviour?
- ✓ How does my partner/child feel loved?
- ✓ How do I show love and care for those important to me?

Be yourself in your way, Strong, Bold, Inspired

Why do you ask yourself "why"?

> *" It's not about what happened to you, but about what you choose to do with what happened to you."*
> Epictetus

It's a natural human tendency to seek explanations for the events and situations we encounter. This search for causality helps us make sense of our experiences, learn from them, and find ways to move forward. However, this pursuit can become problematic when it becomes an obsessive concern, consuming our energy and attention in a neither productive nor healthy way.

When we ask," Why me? " or " Why is this happening to me, something I never imagined? " we often attribute blame for current circumstances to factors or people from our past, whether it's parents, teachers, friends, or partners. While it's true that external influences and past relationships shape our personality and perception to some extent, investing excessive energy in allocating responsibility for the current situation to others can hinder us from taking control and responsibility for our future.

Moreover, this excessive focus on the past and what others have done can create a sense of victimisation, where we feel that we are at the mercy of circumstances and others' behaviour. Even if there is a kernel of truth in our feelings of injustice or pain, staying in this position does not help us grow, evolve, or heal.

The key to overcoming this emotional trap is intentionally orienting ourselves towards the "here and now" moment and the future, focusing on what we can control: our reactions, thoughts, and actions. This means acknowledging the influence of the past on the current situation without allowing it to define who we are or what we can achieve.

Instead, we use past experiences as a learning platform or a catalyst for change and personal growth.

Taking responsibility for our lives and actions allows us to free ourselves from the burden of the past and to move forward with greater clarity and determination towards the future. In this process, it is crucial to seek support and guidance through friends, a therapist, or a support community to navigate life's challenges healthily and constructively.

Instead of getting lost in „why" questions and blaming others, we can choose to ask more powerful and solution-oriented questions, such as „What can I learn from this?" and „How can I move forward in a way that fully honours my values and aspirations?" By directing our energy proactively and positively, we open the path to new possibilities and create our own way towards fulfilment and happiness.

I invite you to reflect: Sometimes we invest a lot, too much energy in seeking explanations and responsibility for what happened to us, and we end up focusing our attention on the past and others:" I am this way because my father or that teacher or my mother did, said... etc. etc. and so on."

The „why" isn't helpful if it keeps us fixated on the past and others, we consider responsible. It's helpful when it offers the perspective to act differently and to learn from painful experiences.

After understanding the value of this "why" in a certain circumstance in your life, ask yourself:

- ✓ What can I do for myself today?
- ✓ How can I become responsible for my present?

Be yourself in your way, Strong, Bold, Inspired

When "no" actually means a resounding "YES" to the life we want

> *"The hard decisions are not about what we do, but about what we give up doing."*
> Steve Jobs

Saying "no" when necessary represents one of the most potent forms of asserting's autonomy and a fundamental pillar in the healthy management of personal boundaries.

The ability to refuse specific requests, invitations, or pressures allows us to manage better our limited resources, such as time, energy, and attention while ensuring that these are directed towards activities and relationships that support our values, goals, and well-being.

However, saying "no" can be extremely difficult for many of us, because there are various psychological and social mechanisms that can hinder this ability:

1. **Fear of rejection:** Many fear their refusal will be interpreted as hostility or disinterest, thus affecting important relationships. In the desire to be liked or accepted, they may be tempted to accept requests not in line with their needs or desires.

2. **Guilt**: The culture in which we grew up can condition us to associate saying "no" with selfishness, triggering feelings of guilt when we try to prioritise our own needs. This mistaken perception can prevent us from setting healthy boundaries.

3. **Social conformity**: The pressure to conform to the norms or expectations of the group can make it difficult to say "no," even when the requests conflict with personal values or desires.

4. **Lack of self-confidence**: Individuals with low self-esteem may have difficulty recognizing their own worth and, therefore, may believe they do not deserve or have the right to express their needs and desires.

5. **Fear of conflict**: Often, we avoid saying "no" because we fear it will create tension or conflict. The desire to maintain peace can lead us to accept more than we can handle or more than we truly want.

Learning to overcome these obstacles is essential for regaining the ability to make choices that align with our priorities and protect our well-being. This process begins with recognising our own needs and values and having the courage to defend them, even when it may make us feel uncomfortable. Saying "no" does not mean we are selfish or uncaring; on the contrary, it is a declaration of authenticity and respect for ourselves and others. Ultimately, a "no" said at the right time protects us from the consequences of a forced "yes."

In practice, developing the ability to say "no" respectfully but firmly can start with small steps—such as refusing minor requests that don't put us in difficult situations—and gradually evolve towards setting stronger boundaries in relationships or in response to major demands. As we become more familiar with and empowered by these experiences, we begin to feel more comfortable setting and defending our boundaries, making room to say "yes" to the life we truly want to live.

I invite you to reflect: If we can't say "no" to some things, we can't make room to say "yes" to others. Sometimes, more often than we care to admit, if we can't say "no" to those around us, we can't say "yes" to our needs. Saying "no" can be challenging because many mechanisms may be ready to block us: focus on them; how do they prevent you from saying no?

Is there any aspect of your life that you can protect through a polite and firm "no"?

What do I want to start saying no to?

Be yourself in your way

How well am I thriving in the garden I'm planted in?

> *"You are the average of the five people you spend the most time with."* – Jim Rohn

The significant influence that the people we choose to spend time with have on us cannot be underestimated. They not only define the quality of our lives through the experiences we share but, in a very real way, shape who we are and who we become. Our relationships can influence our well-being, emotional welfare, decisions, and even the trajectory of our lives. Therefore, it is essential to be aware of these relationships' impact on us and choose our company carefully.

One of the most essential ways relationships enrich our lives is through the feedback, support, and encouragement we give and receive from each other. In a healthy relational environment, this exchange is mutually nourishing. People who inspire, support, and challenge us to grow to help us expand our limits, overcome our fears, and take risks. They can provide the perspective needed to see possibilities we might not have considered and give us the strength to face challenges.

On the other hand, toxic or devaluing relationships can diminish self-esteem, cultivate insecurity, and inhibit personal growth. Individuals who constantly criticise, underestimate, or discourage our ambitions can have a profound negative impact on how we see ourselves and our decisions. Therefore, it is crucial to distinguish between relationships that nourish us and those that deplete us.

Making space for people who nourish us emotionally and spiritually involves understanding our values and developing self-respect. This entails setting healthy boundaries, expecting respect and consideration from those around us, and being willing to distance ourselves from relationships that do not respect these rights.

In an ideal world, we strive to create a mutually beneficial social circle in which each person is both a " feeder" and a "fed. " This means being present, actively listening, and sharing our experiences and wisdom. It's also about asking for help and offering support without expecting anything in return.

Relationships represent the pillars we build around our lives and can profoundly affect how we live and perceive ourselves. Therefore, it is vital to surround ourselves with people who share our values, inspire us, and allow us to grow. This awareness and intentionality in choosing relationships can transform the quality of our life experience and the direction in which it unfolds.

I invite you to reflect: The people we surround ourselves with define the quality of our lives and influence our emotional well-being. That's why it's essential to nurture and be nurtured by these relationships. Take some time to review the people in your life:

- ✓ Who do you want to turn to when you need to cry or when you want to share what makes you happy?

- ✓ What is the characteristic that nourishes you the most about these people?

- ✓ Ask yourself: With whom would I like to spend more time? What is beneficial about their company?

Be yourself in your way, Strong, Bold, Inspired

There will always be uncertainty and unpredictability.

> *"Freedom is not the absence of commitments, but the ability to choose - and commit to - what is best for you."*
> Paulo Coelho

The fear of making choices—especially those that may bind us for a long time—is a universal human trait. This fear stems from our deep desire to avoid regret and not feel constrained by decisions that we might later deem wrong. We tend to view "forever" as a sentence, limiting our freedom to choose and evolve. This feeling is intensified by the awareness that life is unpredictable and constantly changing, and what seems right today may not be so tomorrow.

However, it is essential to recognise that "forever" is more of a mental construct than an absolute reality. Rarely does life bind us to our choices in an irrevocable way. Most decisions can be adjusted, amended, or even reversed as we grow and change. Reality is dynamic, just as we are.

On the other hand, avoiding choices out of fear of commitment and the desire to keep all options open can condemn us to a superficial existence devoid of the depth and fulfilment that only meaningful commitments can provide. A rich life is often the result of courageous choices that define and shape us. Essentially, through a continuous refusal to choose, we risk losing what life has most precious to offer.

This paradox of choice—the fear of being bound by a decision "forever" on the one hand and the recognition that avoiding decisions deprives us of deeply human experiences on the other—prompts us to reevaluate our perspective on choices and commitments.

Choosing means taking a risk but is also an essential step towards self-discovery and living an authentic and fulfilling life.

Therefore, instead of being paralysed by the fear of "forever," adopting a more flexible and open approach to our decisions would be wiser. By embracing uncertainty and unpredictability as intrinsic components of life, we can begin to appreciate the actual value of commitment and the courage to choose. In this sense, it is desirable to be guided by what impassions us, enriches us, and gives us meaning, acknowledging that while some choices may have long-term consequences, we always can adapt and navigate through changes, regardless of their complexity or difficulty.

I invite you to reflect. Often, we are afraid to choose because we fear the consequences of our choices; we are afraid of making mistakes and not being able to go back. We remain stuck "forever". The good news is that" forever" does not exist in nature or reality; the bad news is that if we continue not to choose, we never enjoy. Because of the fear of "forever", we never enjoy, as we postpone the chance to choose and learn from our choices.

What choices am I prevented from making by the fear of binding myself "forever"?

Be yourself in your way, Strong, Bold, Inspired

Too much water can kill a flower.

" You must take care of your health, your own life, your future." Jim Rohn

The assistance and support we offer to loved ones and others are fundamental elements of human relationships. These acts of care are based on empathy, love, and the desire to see those around us thrive. However, there are important nuances in how we choose to offer help, and recognising the difference between being a support and perpetuating dependence can radically change the dynamics of our relationships.

In the case of people, we deeply care about and who depend on us—whether they are family members, partners, or close friends—our sense of responsibility can be both a blessing and a burden. We want to support them and see them overcome obstacles, but there is a delicate balance between helping and allowing the person to learn, grow, and become autonomous. For example, by helping them too much, we risk depriving them of the opportunity to develop their abilities to cope with challenges, implicitly suggesting that they cannot manage life's difficulties on their own.

On the other hand, there are situations where we provide ongoing care to individuals who could potentially manage on their own or who could greatly benefit from taking responsibility for their own lives. The reasons for doing so may vary, from the desire to feel indispensable, to control, or from the fear of being seen as selfish. In these cases, we may unintentionally convey a message that the person in question is not competent or strong enough to navigate life on their own. This dynamic can create a cycle of unhealthy dependence, limiting the potential for both parties to grow and be independent.

The difference between caregiving and fostering autonomous growth often lies in how we practice our intentions and actions. Instead of immediately rushing to solve problems for others, we can offer guidance, emotional support, and encouragement, encouraging them to make their own decisions and face the consequences. This approach not only respects their autonomy and capacity to take responsibility for their own journey but also empowers them to become more resilient and confident in their abilities.

Reflecting on how we choose to help and recognising moments when our support can become more of a hindrance, we can begin to navigate the complexities of human relationships with greater wisdom. By learning to help in a way that encourages autonomy and growth, we enrich our relationships and contribute to others' development towards realising their full potential. True care comes from loving others enough to allow them to stand on their own two feet, even when we most desire to hold their hand.

I invite you to reflect: We often find ourselves helping someone we care about, who depends on us and for whom we feel responsible. Other times, however, we have the same attitude towards people who could be autonomous, but we continue to care for them or confuse closeness and concern with caregiving. Is there someone around you whom you continue to take care of? What responsibility would you like to release? And how can you do this?

Whom do I want to stop "helping"?

Be yourself in your way, Strong, Bold, Inspired

Who am I when nobody is watching?

"Integrity is doing what is right even when no one is watching."
C.S. Lewis

Awareness of how other's perceptions influence our behaviour and decisions is essential in understanding our identity and autonomy. We are social beings, and as such, the perception of others plays a significant role in how we shape our actions and present ourselves to the world. Whether it's the desire to be accepted, not to be judged, or to integrate, we often mould our behaviour to meet societal or close ones' expectations.

In the context of this dynamic, the proposition to imagine ourselves free from the gaze of others opens a universe of possibilities and self-exploration. The question „What would I do if I were sure that no one is watching?" invites us to connect with our deepest desires, often inhibited by fears of judgment or rejection. It allows us to explore aspects of our identity that remain unexpressed due to these fears, reflecting on who we are when we set aside the mask built for social comfort.

This „hunger for freedom", which many of us aspire to, highlights the intrinsic desire for authenticity and unrestricted self-expression. The freedom to be honest with oneself without being limited by unwritten rules or the fear of others' reactions represents the essence of authenticity. At the same time, the restraint we impose on our own expression under the influence of external critical scrutiny often reflects our own internal judgment, the same judgment that makes us censor and limit ourselves.

Confronting this internal duality requires courage and a profound understanding of our values and uniqueness. Accepting and embracing who we truly are, regardless of the potential judgment of others, is an act of self-affirmation and independence. By learning to appreciate our qualities, desires, and imperfections, we can build a life that authentically reflects who we are, not who we believe we should be for others.

As we cultivate this authenticity, we realise that truly valuable freedom does not come from the absence of external gazes but from our internal acceptance. It comes from the power to stand firm in our essence, even under the pressure of others' expectations and judgments. This way of living authentically not only allows us to fulfil our aspirations and desires but also gives those around us a chance to know and appreciate us in our most sincere and unconditional form.

I invite you to reflect: We are all more or less sensitive to the gaze of others. Even when we consider —and even properly consider— this gaze, we often limit or condition ourselves.

Now close your eyes and think: " What would I do if I were sure no one is watching me?"

This desire often speaks to our hunger for freedom, and that restriction we place instead speaks to our critical gaze in the face of the judgment we fear from others.

- ✓ Who am I when no one is watching me?
- ✓ What would I like to do away from the eyes of others?

Be yourself in your way, Strong, Bold, Inspired

I dare to apologise

"To err is human, to forgive, divine."
Alexander Pope

Apologising can be perceived mistakenly as a sign of weakness or defeat, but this action demonstrates courage, maturity, and integrity. When we sincerely apologise, we do not undermine our worth or success; on the contrary, we show that we dare to acknowledge when we have made a mistake and are willing to take responsibility for our actions. Apologising indicates that the relationship and well-being of the other person are important to us and that we care enough to set aside our pride.

Apologising without adding a "but" or offering justifications is crucial to ensure our apologies are perceived as authentic and sincere. Too often, the temptation to add explanations or justifications stems from the desire to protect our image or diminish our mistakes' impact. However, this approach can dilute the message we are trying to convey and can hinder the healing process. By foregoing any "buts," we place ourselves in a vulnerable position, which is true. Still, this vulnerability is what allows the apology to touch the other person's heart and contribute to repairing the rifts between us.

It is important to understand that it is never too late to apologise. The longer we delay this gesture, the greater the risk of allowing uncertainties and pains to persist—both within ourselves and within the other person. Even after a long time, an apology can pave the way for closure and healing of emotional wounds, allowing both parties to move forward in a healthier and more hopeful manner.

However, it is essential to recognize when we are not genuinely ready to apologize. Apologising before feeling genuine remorse or being ready to change our behaviour for the future will neither be convincing nor helpful. In such moments, it is better to take the necessary time to reflect on our actions, their impact, and how we wish to behave differently in the future. By respecting our process and needs, we prepare ourselves for an apology that is not only spoken but also sincerely felt, which can truly bring healing.

I invite you to reflect: Apologizing doesn't mean declaring yourself a failure in front of the other person. It means you regret what happened and you're willing to act differently in the future. Apologizing without adding "buts" helps us connect with others to heal rifts. No matter how much time has passed since the mistake, it's always good to do so; it allows us to close an experience, primarily within ourselves fully. If we're not ready or willing to do this, it's essential to respect our own time and needs.

- ✓ Who would I like to apologise to?
- ✓ What is preventing me from doing it?

Be yourself in your way, Strong, Bold, Inspired

How do you receive compliments?

"Too many people underestimate a well-deserved compliment as something trivial, when in fact, it is a wonderful reward."
Malcolm Forbes

Many people find it challenging to gracefully accept compliments. Despite the giver's good intentions, compliments can trigger a wide range of internal reactions, from discomfort and suspicion to self-deprecation. Though these reactions may seem modest and unassuming, they have roots in the depths of our self-perception and in our relationship with our own self-worth.

Many feel uncomfortable receiving compliments because they place them in the spotlight, generating emotional vulnerability. They fear that they do not deserve this recognition or that the compliment implies an implicit expectation to which they will have to respond. This discomfort can be amplified in cultures where modesty is considered an essential virtue, and pretending to be indifferent to one's praises is seen as a sign of humility.

Another common response to compliments is the tendency to downplay merit with justifications. Phrases like „Oh, it was nothing special" or „Anyone could have done that" are ways to redirect or diminish the value of the recognition given. This behaviour may stem from a need to appear humble or from difficulty in accepting that we could genuinely have done something worthy of praise.

There are situations where compliments are met with self-deprecation or disbelief. This reaction may reflect an internal struggle with low self-esteem, where the individual truly feels they don't deserve the praise received. In other cases, compliments can be met with suspicion, raising questions about the giver's hidden intentions or whether they are genuinely sincere.

Learning to accept compliments gracefully is an essential part of developing self-esteem and embracing our own worth. This begins with recognizing that you deserve praise and appreciation, regardless of the imperfections you may see in yourself or your actions. We must train ourselves to say "Thank you" and let the kind words touch us, fuel our confidence, and inspire us to continue positively.

Compliments, when received in the spirit they are given, can be a powerful catalyst for personal growth and enriching interpersonal relationships. They remind us that we are seen and appreciated and that what we do matters. Thus, the step towards accepting compliments gracefully is, in fact, a step towards fully accepting and embracing our value and contribution to the world around us.

I invite you to reflect. Often, we find it difficult to accept compliments. Sometimes, we feel uncomfortable, tend to justify them, diminish their value, or lack trust in them. What if we trained ourselves to receive them with open arms without adding anything?

- ✓ How do you receive compliments?

Be yourself in your way, Strong, Bold, Inspired

The legacy I leave behind.

> *"I want to leave a mark on the universe, not just survive. If it's about something, I want it to be about the ideas and significance I bring. I want to be remembered for changing something... even if it's not always for the better."* Steve Jobs

Amidst the hustle and bustle of everyday life, it's easy to get absorbed in the constant routine and lose sight of the bigger picture. Our schedules are often filled with tasks and short-term objectives that, while necessary, can distract us from fundamental questions about the meaning and direction of our lives. Questions about „why" and „for what purpose" we do certain things may seem like philosophical luxuries afforded only to those who have „time to spare. "

But this is a misconception. Such questions are essential for living a fulfilled and conscious life.

When we pause to reflect on the direction of our lives and the reasons behind our daily activities, we give ourselves the chance to recalibrate and redirect our actions towards what truly matters to us. This could be discovering a passion we've neglected, renewing our commitment to a long-term goal, or simply confirming that we're on the right path.

Moreover, in moments of reflection and introspection, we can recognise whether our daily activities align with our core values. This alignment is crucial because a significant discrepancy between our values and our actions can lead to stress, frustration, and a sense of unfulfillment.

It's essential to understand that these moments of reflection don't require hours of contemplation and detachment from reality. Reflection can be an active and practical process integrated into daily life. It could mean spending a few minutes each evening thinking about the day's accomplishments and how they align with your long-term goals. It could also mean periodically reassessing your objectives and priorities to ensure they meet your current needs and future aspirations.

Answers to questions about life direction and the source of motivation don't always come easily or quickly. It's a discovery process that can take years and inevitably evolves as we evolve. However, the commitment to seeking these answers and acting following them differentiates a life lived by chance from one lived with intention and purpose.

So, even amidst our busy and responsibility-filled lives, making time to reflect on the direction and meaning we wish to pursue represents an investment in a more fulfilled and significant life. This is how we ensure that we're not just existing but genuinely living to the fullest.

I invite you to reflect: Sometimes, caught up in the frenzy of our daily activities, we're not mindful of the direction of our lives, which is the reason why we do everything we do. These aren't questions to philosophise over and lose us in thought. They're questions we can ask ourselves to focus on:

- ✓ If I could change something in the world, what would it be?
- ✓ How would I like to be remembered by the people I know?
- ✓ What do I want to be remembered for in the world?
- ✓ The answers to these questions likely hold the profound meaning behind everything we do.

Be yourself in your way, Strong, Bold, Inspired

In the end

In the pages of this book, we've embarked on a journey - a quest not of miles but of mindsets in search of the precious peaks of optimism and the tranquil valleys of gratitude. It's an odyssey that requires dedication, an open heart, and an open mind. We understand that, although the path is steep and the thickets are often dense, the pursuit of happiness and positive thinking is worthwhile and achievable.

In this journey, we recognise a straightforward yet challenging truth: to enjoy our aspirations, we must commit to sustained effort and growth. The transformative power of determination is our compass, guiding us through the often-tangled forest of self-doubt and the shaded groves of uncertainty. The critical and encouraging revelation here is that achieving our hopes and dreams is not a distant myth but a real possibility. Like seeds sprouting in fertile soil, our actions and intentions can blossom.

However, what are the tools for this great self-construction? I argue that the foundation begins with cultivating self-confidence—a delicate art that involves tending to the soil of our uncertainty with small yet deliberate actions. Every gesture, every word of self-encouragement, is a brick laid on the path to our temple of self-assurance. As we build, we unlock the potential within us, tapping into the wellspring of qualities that fortify our mental and emotional edifice.

Resilience is one of these qualities - a bastion against life's storms. It's not just about weathering the storms but learning to dance in the rain, to find inner peace amidst the chaos. Alongside resilience, mindfulness stands as a pillar of tranquillity. This practice allows us to be fully present, to embrace each moment as a unique gift, polished by the sands of time. These practices enrich our journey, adding depth and colour to our experiences.

Equally crucial is gratitude, a powerful force that shifts our perspective, allowing us to see beauty in the mundane and learn lessons from hardships. It's an affirmation of our existence, a song that harmonises with the universe's rhythm. By regularly expressing gratitude, we weave a tapestry of positivity that shields us from the cold whispers of negativity.

Self-love is the jewel that crowns our journey. Without it, we are ships without helms, adrift in a tumultuous and unpredictable sea of collective expectations and comparisons. Cultivating self-love involves accepting our flaws, celebrating our strengths, and embarking on the journey of improvement not from self-reproach but from a place of self-respect and goodwill.

However, self-confidence doesn't equate to challenging the world in all its vastness. Instead, it means recognising that our sphere of influence, regardless of its size, is the domain where we can make a difference. It's understanding that self-confidence acts as a catalyst for transformation - internally and in the world around us. With the mantle of self-assurance, the remarkable unfolds within us and spills over into the external, touching others, inspiring change, and creating ripples in the vast ocean of humanity.

Let's cherish the notion that believing in ourselves is the source of greatness. Indeed, remarkable things await us, but perhaps even more importantly, remarkable things await those whom we will influence. As we grow, so does the world alongside us in a harmonious symphony of personal evolution and collective progress.

Be yourself in your way, Strong, Bold, Inspired

Additional resources

We all know that a good book can be more than just an escape from reality; it can be a mentor, a friend, and, last but not least, an endless source of wisdom and inspiration.

Every book we open invites us to explore new ideas, meet memorable characters, and travel to places we may never otherwise see. Furthermore, they open the door to a deeper understanding of ourselves and our world. Through the stories, histories, and perspectives they present, each title I recommend aims to enrich, challenge, and expand the way we see and experience life.

I hope these books will offer you the pleasure of reading and material for thought and reflection. Whether you find in them a refuge, inspiration, or a new perspective, may each page be a window to something valuable and meaningful.

The list could have been very long, but I limited it to just a few books. Indeed, these books will guide your steps towards others.

Brene Brown – The Courage to Be Vulnerable.

Eckhart Tolle – The Power of Now.

Epictetus – The Handbook.

Gary Chapman – The Five Love Languages.

James Clear - Atomic Habits. An Easy and Proven Way to Build Good Habits and Break Bad Ones.

Thich Nhat Hanh - The Miracle Of Mindfulness: The Classic Guide to Meditation by the World's Most Revered Master

ABOUT THE AUTHOR

Felicia Juliana Ursarescu is a dedicated personal and professional development coach with a passion for empowering individuals to live fulfilling lives.

As a certified Professional Coach (B-0264A, Registro Nazionale Coach Professionisti Italia), Hypnotist, and Specialist in Clinical Neuropsychology, Felicia Juliana Ursarescu brings a wealth of knowledge and experience to her work.

She is also the author of several books, Italian and Romanian: "*Le parole non dette*," "*Vindecarea și integrarea copilului interior rănit*," and "*EFT- intră în contact cu propriile emoții și învață să le gestionezi în mod eficient*," which offer practical guidance and transformative techniques for personal growth.

Printed in Great Britain
by Amazon